TARANTO

Taranto

Don Newton & A. Cecil Hampshire

NEW ENGLISH LIBRARY
TIMES MIRROR

First published by William Kimber & Co. Ltd, 1959.
© William Kimber & Co. Ltd, 1959.

*

FIRST NEL PAPERBACK EDITION OCTOBER 1974

*

NEL Books are published by
New English Library Limited from Barnard Inn, Holborn, London, E.C.1.
Made and printed in Great Britain by Hunt Barnard Printing Ltd, Aylesbury, Bucks.

450019926

FOREWORD AND ACKNOWLEDGEMENTS

It is barely fifty years since the strength of the Royal Navy was measured in battleships, and Britannia ruled the waves, with the big gun as her major fleet weapon.

But when Parliament approved the allocation of £35,000 in the 1909 Navy Estimates for the building of a rigid airship a new era in naval development was begun. Although the Navy's first airship in fact came to grief as she was being brought from her hangar for trials, her construction nevertheless foreshadowed the extension of sea power to include the new element of the air.

During the half-century that has elapsed since then there have been many great achievements in the world of aviation. To these the Royal Navy and its airmen have made a considerable contribution.

The first sailors to fly were officers of the British Navy, who, it might be said, took to the air like ducks to water. One of these enthusiasts, Commander Oliver Schwann, developed a hydroplane by private enterprise, and in 1911 became the first man to ascend from water. His initiative and the success of his experiments led to the design in the following year, by a fellow naval officer, of the first seaplane and, a little later, to the birth of the flying boat.

Another naval pioneer, Lieutenant C. R. Samson, flew a biplane off a platform erected over the bows of the battleship *Africa* in 1912. And when in 1917 Squadron Commander E. H. Dunning of the Royal Naval Air Service landed a Sopwith Pup on the deck of the converted cruiser H.M.S. *Furious* he became the first pilot to land an aeroplane on a ship under way, and the development of the aircraft-carrier as we know it today inevitably followed.

Aviation played a significant, though far from decisive, part in the First World War. Naval airmen attacked and destroyed German Zeppelins, patrolled confined waters in search of U-boats, and acted as spotters for the guns of the Fleet. During the Dardanelles campaign the first aerial torpedo was successfully launched against an enemy surface ship by Flight Commander

C. H. K. Edmonds of the Royal Naval Air Service. It was not until the Second World War that air power at sea was fully demonstrated.

Until then it was firmly believed, except by the most ardent and far-sighted enthusiasts, that an enemy fleet could only be effectively attacked within the range of guns. No navy had ever attempted to destroy a fleet with aircraft. Nevertheless these 'fanatics,' as they were dubbed, strove tirelessly for recognition of the potential striking power of the Fleet Air Arm. But deeds, not words, were needed to convince the sceptics that aircraft could become more lethal than guns.

Proof was forthcoming on the night of November 11th, 1940, when the crews of a handful of flimsy, slow-flying aeroplanes, which had been flown off an aircraft-carrier at sea 170 miles away, inflicted more damage on the Italian battle fleet, lying snugly at anchor behind the powerful defences of its base at Taranto, than the German Navy suffered in daylight at the Battle of Jutland.

By superb airmanship and the faultless execution of a brilliantly conceived plan, they not only surprised and crippled the Italian fleet, but altered the course of the war in the Mediterranean, shattered a dictator's dream, and laid the foundation for ultimate Allied victory in North Africa.

Until that memorable night in 1940 Britain had been suffering an almost unbroken run of defeats. Alone and well nigh friendless, threatened with invasion from the sea and air, she sorely needed a victory. The Fleet Air Arm gave it to her. The Navy's airmen did more. They put naval aviation on the map.

In telling the first full story, from all sources, of that brilliant and daring attack, we wish to acknowledge the generous help and encouragement we have received from those who either took part, or were concerned in some way with the operation.

Lastly we would like to emphasise that any opinions expressed in this book are our own and do not represent official views, or those of anyone else.

D. N. & A. C. H.

CONTENTS

*Victory is not a name strong
enough for such a scene.*

NELSON

CHAPTER I

THE PLAN

A SMARTLY handled naval motor-boat, with the White Ensign fluttering at her stern, foamed alongside the towering grey-painted bulk of His Majesy's aircraft-carrier *Glorious*, anchored in Alexandria harbour.

From it stepped the trim, white-uniformed figure of Captain Lumley Lyster, the warship's commander. Hastily he mounted the steps of the accommodation ladder, and paused briefly at the head of the gangway to acknowledge the respectful salute of the Officer of the Watch.

'Get hold of Commander Willoughby and Commander Mackintosh,' he ordered, 'and ask them to come along to my cabin at once.'

'Aye, aye, sir.'

As the captain hurried below, the lieutenant crooked a beckoning finger at the gangway messenger. A moment later the young seaman doubled away on his errand, and the Officer of the Watch turned to level his telescope at the British Mediterranean Fleet flagship in the battleship anchorage across the harbour, from which the captain had just returned.

'The Old Man seems to be in a bit of a flap,' he mused. 'Wonder if the balloon's gone up at last?'

Lyster's haste matched the urgency of the moment.

It was September, 1938, and Europe had been thrown into a crisis by the threatening attitude of Chancellor Adolf Hitler towards Germany's neighbour, Czechoslovakia. The cause of the friction was Hitler's support of the noisy clamour for 'self-determination' of Czeckoslovakia's Sudeten-German minorities.

An anxious Britain had warned Germany of the consequences of any attempt to solve this problem by the use of force. Then, taking an unprecedented step in international diplomacy, Prime Minister Neville Chamberlain had on his own initiative flown to Germany to discuss the Sudeten-German question with the Chancellor in person.

But when his plane touched down at Munich airport he was greeted by the news that Konrad Henlein, Hitler's henchman in Czechoslovakia, secretly egged on by his master, was truculently demanding no less than the absorption of the Sudetenland into the Nazi Reich.

Chamberlain achieved little. Hitler was determined upon the liquidation of Czechoslovakia as an essential step in his plans for the establishment of a Greater German Reich. He was confident that the Western democracies would no more spring to her aid than they had raised a finger to prevent his re-occupation of the Rhineland and the recent brutally accomplished subjugation of Austria.

Convinced, however, that Hitler could be dissuaded from plunging the world into war, Chamberlain hurried back to London and summoned a Cabinet meeting to consider the German demands.

Then, carrying with him Anglo-French proposals for the cession of the Sudetenland to the Reich to which the Czechs had been forced to agree, he flew again to see the Fuehrer at Godesberg. But Hitler cynically increased his demands.

The talks broke down, and the disillusioned British Prime Minister returned to London in an atmosphere of gloom and foreboding.

Earlier in a prescient speech to his constituents at Theydon Bois, Winston Churchill had warned the nation that 'the world is steadily moving to a climax which cannot be long delayed'.

War clouds gathered over Europe as Hitler stepped up his campaign of vilification against the unhappy Czechs.

Precautions against air attack were taken in Britain. Air-raid trenches were dug in Hyde Park; press notices instructed householders how to build garden shelters to protect themselves against falling bombs; London's balloon barrage was tested, and the silvery shapes of the tethered gasbags floated over the apprehensive capital. In France army reserves were called up and the Maginot Line was manned.

In both countries the prudent, the anxious and the cowardly packed their bags for an indefinite stay abroad.

The *Glorious* had been in harbour at Malta with the rest of the Mediterranean Fleet when the crisis broke. As the tension heightened a secret warning signal was flashed from the Admiralty in London, and the British warships sailed from Malta's Grand Harbour and headed eastward for Alexandria.

It had long been recognised by the Navy that Malta would speedily become untenable as the Mediterranean Fleet's main base in the event of a war which included a hostile Italy. And if war should break out against Germany, Mussolini, Hitler's Axis partner, could not be expected to remain aloof.

Italian air and naval forces would swoop upon Malta in an attempt to sever Britain's Mediterranean lifeline.

Four days after Chamberlain's first visit to Hitler the Duce had issued a sinister warning of his intentions.

'In the event of war,' he trumpeted from the balcony of the Palazzo Venezia, in Rome, 'Italy's position is already chosen.'

On arrival at the Egyptian port the Commander-in-Chief of the Mediterranean Fleet, Admiral Sir Dudley Pound, summoned his captains to the flagship, the battleship *Warspite*. Seated with them around a table in his day cabin, Pound defined the strategy he proposed to adopt should Italy join with Germany in the conflict that now loomed nearer every hour.

To the Royal Navy Italy had been regarded as the potential enemy in the Mediterranean ever since Mussolini led his Fascists to power in 1922. His sabre-rattling rantings and the speedy growth of the Italian armed forces had clearly shown that the aim of the Italian dictator was national aggrandisement.

In 1935 came dramatic proof when, without a shred of justification, Italy attacked and subjugated Abyssinia. The Duce dreamed of a revived Roman Empire.

'We must hit the Italian fleet at once and as hard and often as we can,' Admiral Pound bluntly told his officers.

To Lyster the admiral disclosed the special role he had in mind for the *Glorious*.

It was Pound's conviction that once Mussolini's massive air strength was deployed against her the life of his carrier would be brief. But she could perhaps strike one effective blow before she was overwhelmed.

He directed Lyster to examine the feasibility of an air assault on the Italian fleet in its own harbours; to prepare a plan accordingly; and to be ready to carry out the plan 'when the whistle blows'.

It was this directive that had sent Lyster hurrying back to his ship. Such an attack as the Commander-in-Chief proposed was without parallel in naval warfare. Yet Lyster had no doubts that its execution was well within the capabilities of his air squadrons. And an outline plan for precisely this operation was in fact already in existence.

When he assumed command of the *Glorious* Lyster had discovered among her secret files a paper prepared three years previously when Britain and Italy had teetered on the edge of war as a result of Mussolini's wanton attack on Abyssinia. The document contained draft proposals for an air attack by British naval planes upon the Italian fleet in its own strongholds.

Commanders Guy Willoughby and Lachlan Mackintosh, the two officers Lyster had summoned to his cabin, held the appointments respectively of Senior Fleet Air Arm Officer and Senior Observer in the carrier. Both were flyers of long experience, and under their tuition the air squadrons of the *Glorious* had already reached a high standard of performance.

But, along with other naval airmen of their day, Willoughby and Mackintosh were only too well aware that the Fleet Air Arm was the Cinderella of the Service, relegated as much by prejudice as lack of vision in exalted quarters to a minor role in naval warfare. They longed for an opportunity to put naval aviation fairly and squarely on the map. The darkening international scene and the looming threat of war might provide that opportunity.

As they entered the captain's cabin a shaft of sunlight streaming through the open scuttle highlighted a chart of the central Mediterranean which lay on Lyster's desk. The sight riveted their eyes.

'By God, I believe this is it!' thought Willoughby, grimly exultant. 'A chance to show what our lads can do at last.'

He was not disappointed. Briefly the captain outlined the directive from the Commander-in-Chief for a detailed plan to be prepared immediately for an air thrust at the very heart of Fascist sea power. Lyster stabbed with his finger at a point on the chart before him.

'This will be the objective,' he told them. 'The Italian fleet in their main base at Taranto.'

Thus briefed, Willoughby and Mackintosh set to work and, using the 1935 paper as a basis, hammered out their proposed plan of attack.

The tactical conception of the operation presented no insuperable difficulties for squadrons as highly skilled as theirs. Ever since the *Glorious* had recommissioned for service in the Mediterranean back in January of that year, flying training had taken precedence over every other requirement; and the crews of the carrier's strike aircraft had been drilled to a hair in the techniques of bombing and torpedo attacks both by day and at night.

At sea exercises were carried out against stationary and moving targets. Periodic swoops were made on to Malta's Grand Harbour to accustom aircrews to face the intimidating barrage – although only simulated – of shore defences.

When the fleet had moved to its war station, exercises had been stepped up. Nor were they conducted without hazard. Only a few days previously six aircrew had perished in a mid-air collision. But training went on relentlessly.

Analysis of the exercises had proved the theory that air attacks made at night were likely to achieve greater success with fewer casualties than any daylight assault. Emphasis was therefore shifted to night flying, and a third of all the air training in the *Glorious* took place after dark. Her fighter pilots, too, were taught the technique of deck landing at night, an unusual feat in those pre-war days.

As the weeks went by Numbers 812, 823 and 825 Fleet Air Arm Squadrons of H.M.S. *Glorious* had become very proficient indeed. Soon when asked by Home Air Command, 'Who are your night flying squadrons?' Lyster was able to signal the succinct reply, 'All.' His pilots were in fact ahead of their time.

To enable Willoughby and Mackintosh to work out their plan to the smallest detail they needed information about Taranto itself. The reference books on board were not much help. But here Lyster himself was able to come to their assistance. He knew the Italian port well, for he had served as a young lieutenant in the battleship *Queen* when she and other units of the Royal Navy had operated with the Italian fleet from Taranto in the First World War. Thus the blanks were filled in, and the draft plan was given the seal of Lyster's approval.

In Admiral Pound's cabin on board the flagship next day the plan was exhaustively studied by senior staff officers of the Fleet. Everyone agreed that the attack should be made at night. Since Taranto was the Italian Navy's principal base – the Portsmouth of Italy – the anti-aircraft defences of the port were bound to be numerous and powerful and a daylight swoop was obviously out of the question.

There was also full agreement that torpedo-carrying aircraft should form the main striking force. These could be supported by bombers to attack land targets, but their main purpose would be to divert the defences and create confusion in the enemy's midst.

From the early days of naval flying the British Admiralty had considered the torpedo to be the most effective weapon for seaborne aircraft. The first British aviator to launch a torpedo from the air had been a naval officer back in 1914. He was Lieutenant Longmore of the Royal Naval Air Service (now Air Chief Marshal Sir Arthur Longmore, RAF). A year later Flight Commanders Edmonds and Dacre of the RNAS, flying Short 184 seaplanes, proved its effectiveness as an aerial weapon by torpedoing some Turkish merchantmen during the Dardanelles campaign.

Spearhead of the proposed Taranto assault would therefore be Fairey Swordfish torpedo-bombers, with which in 1938 most front-line squadrons of the Fleet Air Arm were equipped.

For reasons of economy, as well as simplicity of handling in the limited space of an aircraft-carrier, the Swordfish had been designed as a multi-purpose aircraft; its full designation being Torpedo-Bomber-Spotter-Reconnaissance (TBSR). The machine was a three-seater biplane with an open cockpit, of steel tube and duralumin construction, with fabric wings which folded and a fixed undercarriage interchangeable with floats. One 650–690-h.p. Bristol Pegasus, 9-cylinder radial air-cooled engine gave a maximum speed of approximately 130 m.p.h., with a cruising speed of something approaching 100 knots.

The armament comprised a Vickers .303-inch machine gun firing through the airscrew, and a Lewis gun fitted at the back of the rear cockpit. The Swordfish could carry a useful load of some 1,800 lb. consisting either of a torpedo or bombs, and its endurance was about five hours. The plane was easy to fly and extremely manoeuvrable. But it was heavy on the stick when diving at high speed since there were no powered controls for aircraft in those days.

Introduced into operational service in 1936, the Swordfish was well liked by Fleet Air Arm pilots. Nevertheless they dubbed it the 'Stringbag' due, they alleged, to the bits and pieces which went into its construction. Destined to serve continuously for a stormier decade than its designers could have visualised, the Swordfish was to earn undying fame before it finally became a museum exhibit. During the war pilots discovered almost without surprise that pieces could be shot off a Stringbag and it would still fly!

To Admiral Pound the hazards involved in striking at a powerful enemy fleet in its own defended port, even under cover of darkness, seemed to be immense. For at that date in history the use of air power alone as a strategic weapon had never been tested, and the risks involved could only be guessed at.

Events in the Spanish Civil War and, to a lesser extent, in

the Sino-Japanese conflict had proved that ships in harbour could be attacked with bombs with reasonable accuracy.

But modern naval anti-aircraft gunnery was highly efficient, and multi-barrelled weapons were now coming into service. Casualties, considered Pound, could be reckoned to amount to as high as fifty per cent of the force engaged, even though the attack would take place at night when the airmen stood their best chance of success.

Willoughby listened to the staff discussion impatiently. He knew that his aircrews nursed a sublime faith in their ability to hit the enemy in his own stronghold and get away again. He shared their optimism, for he had flogged them through their training with just such an operation in view. When his opinion was finally sought by the admiral he was uncompromising.

'The attack will succeed, sir,' he stated flatly, 'with a loss of not more than ten per cent *from all causes.*'

The Commander-in-Chief stared at the airman, impressed by his confidence. Then without further hesitation Pound gave his decision.

'Very well, the plan is accepted,' he told Lyster. 'I think hostilities are inevitable,' he went on. 'If you're smart you can catch the Italian fleet the moment war is declared.'

For Captain Lyster and his airmen the decision made by Admiral Pound was a notable and, as events were to show, an historic recognition of the potential striking power of British naval aircraft. Yet to the Commander-in-Chief the Taranto attack represented only one of the possibilities to be considered in his overall plans to retain control of the Mediterranean. But it was the most promising.

The essence of war is surprise. Therefore if such an unexpected blow could be successfully struck at the Italians at the outset of hostilities the whole balance of naval power in the Mediterranean might well be decisively altered at a stroke.

For Mussolini's fleet was numerically strong, although its fighting qualities had still to be tested. From a couple of obsolete battleships, seven old cruisers and a handful of ageing destroyers in 1922, the Italian Navy had become a force to be reckoned with.

In service in 1938 were two newly reconstructed, 25,000-ton, 27-knot battleships, and another pair were being similarly modernised. Italian shipyards were about to turn out two new and powerful 35,000-tonners, the *Littorio* and *Vittorio Veneto.*

Three more capital ships of the same class had recently been laid down.

Twenty-three cruisers were in commission, eight of them fast, heavily gunned, 10,000-ton ships; and none more than eight years old. There were 128 destroyers on the active list of the Italian Navy, a quarter of them fully fitted for mine-laying; and more than a hundred submarines. A further 20,000 tons were building for Mussolini's undersea fleet.

To meet this Fascist threat Admiral Pound could deploy only three ageing battleships of First World War vintage, five cruisers, twenty-nine destroyers, seven submarines, and a handful of auxiliary craft.

The total air-striking power of his fleet was centred in the *Glorious*, which carried forty-eight front-line aircraft formed into four squadrons. One of these, No. 802, could put a dozen Nimrod and Osprey fighters into the air, both obsolescent types of plane; the other three squadrons, Nos. 812, 823 and 825, were equipped with twelve Swordfish apiece.

In the event of war with the Axis Powers, Admiral Pound's ships and his meagre air squadrons, backed up by whatever shore-based RAF aircraft might be available, would have to face a powerful Navy able to dominate the central Mediterranean, supported by massive air forces operating from the Italian mainland, from Libya and the Dodecanese; while the Suez Canal, which it was his task to protect, could be threatened from Italian air bases along the Red Sea coast.

There was also the possibility of German intervention in the Mediterranean.

The Commander-in-Chief was well aware that his chances of reinforcement from the United Kingdom or elsewhere were slight, since British naval strength would at once be stretched to the limit to cover its global commitments.

Representing one-fifth of the Royal Navy's total operational carrier strength at that time, the *Glorious* was already more than twenty-two years old in 1938. Along with her sisters *Courageous* and *Furious*, she had been laid down in 1916 as an 18-inch gun cruiser under the Emergency First World War building programme. Their design was the brainchild of Admiral Fisher, then First Sea Lord.

All three were converted to aircraft-carriers in the early post-war years; the *Glorious* being the last of the trio to join the fleet in this new role, having completed her long-drawn-out conversion in 1930. She displaced 22,500 tons and, like the

Courageous, had a free flight deck, an 'island' on the starboard side, and one funnel. The *Furious* differed from her sisters, being a complete flat-top with neither funnel nor 'island'.

Of the other two carriers in service in 1938, the *Eagle*, then serving in the Far East but destined to render gallant service in the Mediterranean, was even older. Originally intended for the Chilean Navy as the battleship *Almirante Cochrane*, work on her had ceased at the outbreak of the First World War. In 1917 the British Government purchased the ship from Chile at a cost of more than a million pounds and altered her design to an aircraft-carrier. When she was eventually completed in 1923 she displaced 26,400 tons, could steam at a top speed of twenty-four knots and carried a complement of twenty-one aircraft.

H.M.S. *Hermes*, last and most recently built of all five, had until 1935 enjoyed the distinction of being the only vessel in the British Navy actually designed as an aircraft-carrier. But she was small and slow, carried a complement of only fifteen aircraft, and was herself already nearly twenty years old.

Nearing completion at Birkenhead, however, was a new carrier, twice the size of the *Hermes*, embodying in her great bulk all the improvements experience had taught. Named *Ark Royal*, she was to become one of the Navy's most famous ships. But in September 1938, the *Ark* was still in her fitting-out yard.

The *Glorious* and her seagoing sisters lacked such modern refinements as catapults, crash barriers - other than a primitive form of 'safety barrier' – indeed any of the landing aids which have become commonplace today. Flying-off could only be accomplished by steaming the ship at top speed into the wind – a manoeuvre which in war rendered a carrier vulnerable to hostile submarine attack. Deck landing control by means of a batsman had recently been adopted, but only by one squadron in the *Courageous*, and pilots were not bound to obey his signals. Aircraft landing-on were jerked to a standstill by means of arrester wires with far less efficiency than in the carriers of today and nets were always rigged at either side of the flight deck during flying operations to prevent planes from crashing over the side if their pilots made a bad landing.

Yet if the Royal Navy's air strength was not as numerous or as powerful as it might have been, the British Mediterranean Fleet possessed in the *Glorious* a class of ship completely lacking in the Fascist Navy.

'Italy is herself a huge aircraft-carrier,' declared the Duce, who had banned his Navy from possessing its own air arm, and he stifled the dissatisfied mutterings of his admirals by permitting catapult planes to be carried in the fleet's battleships and cruisers. But these machines were manned by Air Force flyers who had no conception of the peculiarities of naval requirements. Air Force personnel also manned the reconnaissance aircraft used for naval purposes.

The Royal Navy, too, had suffered for years from lack of control of its own air arm. In 1918 the Royal Naval Air Service, a force of some 55,000 officers and men with 3,000 aircraft, which had originally been created in 1912, had been merged with the Royal Flying Corps, to form the Royal Air Force.

Six years later a separate Fleet Air Arm was formed, but for nearly two decades its administration was shared by the Air Ministry and the Admiralty. The Air Ministry continued to be responsible for the maintenance of naval aircraft and the training of aircrews, and also undertook to provide the Fleet Air Arm with new aircraft of such types and numbers as the Admiralty should specify.

Due to the limited funds the Admiralty was able to allocate to new production, however, the Fleet Air Arm lagged behind the RAF both in design and quantity. Between 1929 and 1932, for instance, only eighteen new planes were added to Fleet Air Arm strength. As previously stated, the demands of economy and the difficulties of handling and maintaining a large number of different types of aircraft afloat led to the design of machines capable of performing more than one function. Hence the evolution of the spectacularly successful Fairy Swordfish.

In 1937 the Admiralty had at last won back complete control of its air arm. But the changeover could only be effected gradually. In 1938 some thirty per cent of Fleet Air Arm pilots belonged to the Royal Air Force, and naval airmen were still required to hold RAF as well as naval commissions before they were permitted to fly. Ground crews were also to a large extent RAF personnel; later on many of these technicians were allowed to turn over to the Navy.

During its lean years the Fleet Air Arm suffered not only by reason of divided control and the economies which were forced upon it, but also from conservatism within the Navy itself.

Gunnery officers were loath to admit the possibility that fleet actions might one day be fought by aircraft alone without the aid of surface ship weapons. For years official opinion refused to budge from the view that the most effective use of naval aircraft was as spotters for the guns of the fleet.

When the RNAS was first formed in 1912, naval aircraft were officially allotted five specific functions. These were to reconnoitre enemy harbours; to search for hostile ships at sea; to hunt submarines; to detect minefields; and to direct the guns of the fleet.

More than a quarter of a century later these functions remained almost unaltered, except that naval aircraft were additionally required to reconnoitre and shadow the enemy at sea, and attack and slow down fast hostile ships which were endeavouring to avoid battle.

But by 1938 the long-held opinion that Fleet Air Arm aircraft were quite incapable of striking a decisive blow at an enemy by themselves was veering. And one of the officers who believed whole-heartedly in the future of the Navy's air arm was Captain Lyster of the *Glorious*.

'There is nothing the air cannot do and nothing can be done without the air,' he had declared on more than one occasion.

Of average height, broadly built, tough and aggressive in outlook, and with something of the Beatty touch about him, Arthur Lumley St George Lyster, CVO, DSO, was in fact himself a gunnery specialist, but with none of the bigotry that characterised so many of his colleagues in that branch.

Born twelve years before the turn of the century, he joined the Navy at the age of fourteen, and was a lieutenant of five years seniority when the First World War began. He served in large and small ships throughout that conflict, and in 1919 was awarded the DSO for good services as gunnery officer of the light cruiser *Cassandra*.

After promotion to captain in 1928, further seagoing posts and a tour of duty at the Admiralty followed. In January 1938, he was appointed to command of the *Glorious* when the carrier recommissioned for further service with the Mediterranean Fleet.

Now he was charged with the task of launching one of the most audacious assaults in history by a method hitherto untried. Its success might lift him to the peak of his career.

But on September 29th, while Europe shivered on the brink of war, Premier Chamberlain flew yet again to see Hitler, accompanied this time by Daladier, the French Prime Minister.

Appeasement was to be the order of the day.

At Munich, where the meeting with the German Dictator took place, Mussolini now strutted importantly in the role of peacemaker. Then, while the world held its breath, the British Prime Minister flew back to London triumphantly waving a piece of paper which bore Hitler's signature.

Since the Western statesmen had supinely given way to his demands, the Fuehrer had seen no objection in subscribing in his turn to a meaningless declaration that Britain and Germany were resolved never again to go to war with one another.

'It's peace with honour,' Chamberlain told the wildly cheering throngs in Downing Street.

The British Fleet was demobilised; the defenders of the Maginot Line returned to their homes. The Taranto plan went back into the secret files of the *Glorious*. German troops goose-stepped into the Sudetenland.

Duff Cooper, First Lord of the Admiralty, resigned in disgust. 'Munich,' he declared, 'sticks in my throat.'

Growled Winston Churchill sombrely, 'We have sustained a defeat.'

All that Britain had gained was time.

Early in 1939 Admiral Pound flew to London to place before the Board of Admiralty new strategical plans to meet the eventuality of war with Nazi Germany and Fascist Italy.

When, a few months later, he was called upon to succeed in office the ailing First Sea Lord, Admiral of the Fleet Sir Roger Backhouse, he took with him the draft outlines of certain operations he had devised for the Mediterranean Fleet to carry out in the event of war. One of these was a naval air attack upon Italian warships in their bases at Taranto and Augusta.

Although Pound held the view that the best people to attack ships were sailors who lived in them, he did not entirely share Lyster's faith in the potentialities of the Navy's air arm. To his written approval of the plan for assaulting the Italian Fleet from the air he had added the words, 'Unless, as I hope, shore-based aircraft will be available for this.'

Events, however, were to prove otherwise.

CHAPTER II

ITALY TAKES THE PLUNGE

THE time that Chamberlain had gained at Munich was brief indeed, for Hitler's faithlessness was soon to be revealed in all its ugly reality.

On March 14th, 1939, in flagrant violation of the Munich Agreement, he annexed the whole of Czechoslovakia, which country he brutally announced had therefore ceased to exist.

On Good Friday, less than a fortnight later – a date which shocked the Christian world nearly as much as the deed itself – Mussolini invaded Albania.

The Dictators were on the march.

Then, while the Czechs were being ruthlessly trampled under the Nazi jackboot, a similar sickening campaign of vilification such as that stricken nation had endured was launched from Berlin against the next victim on Hitler's list, this time Poland.

But there was to be no more appeasement. As the Nazi war of nerves was stepped up, Britain and France prepared to honour their obligations to the threatened Poles.

Nevertheless the Fuehrer was not to be checked. Staking everything on a lightning blow, he hurled his legions across the Polish border on the morning of September 1st, 1939. Warsaw and other Polish cities erupted in the flame and smoke of unheralded Luftwaffe bombs. Two days later the British and French ultimatums to Germany expired, and the second world conflict had begun.

Yet in spite of Mussolini's many bellicose speeches, Italy did not at once join hands with her Axis partner. In fact, in August the Duce had suggested that a world peace conference should be held, at which he doubtless hoped to gain certain material advantages without effort. Hitler brusquely rejected the proposal.

But there was no sincerity behind Mussolini's suggestion. He knew that his country was neither militarily nor economically ready for war. Secretly the two Dictators had agreed that until Italy could accumulate sufficent stocks of munitions and raw materials she should remain neutral.

Accordingly Mussolini waited patiently throughout the winter of 1939-40, while the Nazis swiftly stamped out the last vestiges of resistance in devastated Poland; and in the West Allied and German forces faced each other in that curious twilight period of inactivity known as the 'phoney war'.

His interest quickened when in April 1940, Hitler treacherously attacked and overran Denmark and Norway; and he jubilantly greeted the defeat and retirement of the Allied Expeditionary Force in its efforts to aid the Norwegians.

Then when the German armies launched their blitzkrieg against the Low Countries, outflanked the Maginot Line, and drove through to the Channel coast, the Duce was filled with false courage. The moment for which he had been waiting was at hand.

The British were hurled back to the sea at Dunkirk; the French armies shattered and disorganised. Nothing could suit his malevolent intentions better.

Foreseeing some of the events that were about to befall, he had in fact on May 13th informed Count Ciano, his son-in-law and confidant, that he would declare war on Britain and France within a month of that date. On May 29th his official decision to do so on any suitable date after June 5th was communicated to the Italian Chiefs of Staff.

In the meantime the walls of buildings in Italian cities became plastered with posters abusing the Allies in scurrilous language. Statements were published daily in the Fascist press that 'the hour when the order will be given to march is now imminent.'

In provocative speeches Mussolini boasted that five English towns would be bombed for every Italian town, and that an attack on Rome would be followed by an attack on London. 'England,' declared the Duce, 'is Europe's Enemy Number One.'

On June 8th, 1940, all Italian merchant ships on the high seas were ordered to seek shelter in neutral ports. Two days later Mussolini addressed a vast throng from the balcony of the Palazzo Venezia.

'Fighters of the land, the sea and the air, Blackshirts of the revolution and of the legions, men and women of Italy, of the Empire and other Kingdom of Albania, listen!' he declaimed with arrogantly out-thrust jaw. 'The hour marked out by destiny is sounding in the sky of our country This is the hour of irrevocable decisions. We are going to war against the plutocratic and reactionary democracies of the West who have hindered the advance and often threatened the existence of the Italian people.'

Then amid frenzied cheers he announced that declarations of war had already been handed to the British and French Ambassadors.

That night Italian bombers raided Malta.

But there were many people in Italy who bewilderedly asked each other *Perchè*?

Why indeed. For by his action, which brought upon him the contempt and indignation of the free world, Mussolini had condemned his nation to eventual defeat and despair, and himself to an ignoble end.

But the Duce remained unaffected by world opinion. He had chosen the right moment for intervention and Italy had nothing to lose, he thought. The war would be over in three months. Along with Hitler he believed that hostilities would be quickly brought to an end by the Nazi invasion of England in Operation 'Sea Lion,' which was then planned to take place in August; or by aerial assault, or an all-out blow against British shipping.

It was unthinkable that Italy should be left out of these events which might well, as Hitler predicted, 'decide the fate of Europe for a thousand years.' In a mere matter of weeks, he promised his deluded people, Fascist troops would be marching shoulder to shoulder with their Nazi comrades through Trafalgar Square, while inside Buckingham Palace itself he and Hitler would be dictating peace terms.

But this overweening confidence was by no means reflected in the high command of the Italian Navy. There were in fact few Fascists within its ranks, and they did not find it so easy to hate the British. Had not the two navies fought side by side in the First World War?

Within two days of being informed by Marshal Badoglio, Chief of the Italian General Staff, of the decision of the Duce to intervene in the war when and where he chose, Admiral Domenico Cavagnari, Chief of the Italian Naval Staff, was forecasting disaster for his country.

The British Fleet, he wrote in a memorandum to the ebullient Dictator, was superior and in a position to replace its losses rapidly, whereas the Italian Navy could not rely on reinforcement. Secondly, he pointed out, Britain would cease to use the Mediterranean as a supply route, and no action would therefore be possible against her merchant shipping in that sea. Thirdly, without adequate air support for its operations the Italian fleet would be forced to adopt defensive tactics.

The reasons for Cavagnari's pessimism were not far to seek. At an Italo-German naval conference held at Fredrichshaven in June 1939, no concrete agreement had been reached on the subject of mutual assistance between the two countries in the event of war. It was not until much later that Hitler directed that there should be closer co-operation between the armed forces of Germany and Italy. But even this implied that operations would be conducted independently.

In fact, when Italy entered the war no effective preparations for military co-peration had been made between the German and Italian Supreme Commands.

In 1939 the objectives of the Italian Army in the event of war had been outlined by the then Chief of the Italian General Staff, General Pariani. The elimination of the French was given first priority, and against operations the British in Egypt and Somaliland regarded as of secondary importance.

This strategy had been based on the assumption that Spain would enter the war as an Axis partner. In such circumstances the central Mediterranean would become an exclusive Italian naval theatre, sealed off from the West by minefields and defended in the East by the Italian fleet.

But now the situation was changed. The strategic value of the land campaign in North Africa was to be given the highest priority as a major contribution to a German assault on Britain.

All Italian naval forces, wrote Cavagnari, would need to be assigned to the task of guarding the sea routes between Italy and North Africa. Thus the fleet would have to remain on the defensive, using its small ships for convoy duties and basing the larger units in a central position. Yet Mussolini, as Supreme Commander of Italy's armed forces, had directed that operations were to be conducted offensively at sea and in the air, and defensively on land!

As to its air strength, the Italian Navy at the outbreak of war could dispose of only 123 Air Force manned reconnaissance planes and 38 shipborne aircraft. Of the reconnaissance machines the majority were single-engined and of low performance. Barely a score were multi-engined and capable of longer endurance. With the later addition of 48 three-engined bombers to this force the Italian Navy was expected to provide adequate air cover for itself and its operations over the whole expanse of the Mediterranean.

But in spite of Cavagnari's protestations Mussolini was not to be deflected from his purpose. He was abysmally ignorant of the importance of sea power, and had declared, 'I don't know anything about naval matters, so I leave the Navy to take care of itself.'

Convinced that hostilities would be short-lived, he even compelled the transfer to the Air Force and to civilian industry of 300,000 tons of fuel oil, leaving the Navy a meagre stockpile of barely a million and a half tons out of which to provide for a wartime consumption of 200,000 tons monthly.

Nevertheless in 1940 the strength of the Italian Navy was considerable compared with that of the British Mediterranean Fleet. Two of the new 35,000-ton battleships, *Littorio* and *Vittorio Veneto*, faster and more up-to-date than anything the British Navy could boast, were due to come into service in July. The building of two more vessels of the same class, the *Impero* and *Roma*, was being speeded up. With their completion the Italians would dispose of eight powerful capital ships.

When, at the end of May, Marshal Badoglio communicated to Cavagnari Mussolini's directive to be ready to go into action by June 5th, the Chief of the Naval Staff was already fully prepared so far as resources allowed.

The Italian fleet had been on a mobilized footing since as far back as 1935 when the Abyssinian venture was projected, and it had remained at war strength ever since. The morale of its officers and men was high and they were confident of acquitting themselves favourably against their redoubtable opponents.

To the rest of the world when Italy declared war, Britain seemed to be facing hopeless odds. Defeated in Norway, her Expeditionary Force on the Continent snatched from annihilation only by the miracle of Dunkirk; the Channel ports in enemy hands for the first time in a hundred years; threatened by Hitler with air bombardment and invasion; her end must surely be in sight.

Mussolini had no doubt whatever that he could sweep the remnants of the British Navy from the Mediterranean and transform that sea into an Italian lake. As for Malta, he boasted that his fleet and his air force could destroy the place in forty-eight hours.

II

From the beginning of the war the Royal Navy was kept hard at work upon its traditional tasks: transporting troops to France, Norway and the Middle East; organising convoys; instituting a contraband control system for the enforcement of the blockade against Germany; hunting U-boats, and disposing its available ships to guard the far-flung trade routes of the British Empire.

When it became known that a number of German surface warships had reached the open seas before the commencement of hostilities, special raider hunting groups had to be formed to scour the oceans in seach of these marauders.

During this period the Mediterranean Fleet had little to do. Then when it became clear that Mussolini intended to remain neutral, at any rate for the time being, the fleet was denuded of some of its strength.

Cruisers and destroyers were brought home for re-deployment. The battleship *Malaya* and the Mediterranean Fleet's only aircraft-carrier, the *Glorious*, were despatched to the Indian Ocean to take part in the hunt for enemy surface raiders. With the latter went the aircraft and their highly trained crews with which in 1938 Admiral Pound had planned to attack the Italian Navy in its own harbours 'when the whistle blows'.

Day after day Swordfish from the *Glorious* took off to search the sunlit tropical seas from dawn to dusk, hoping to catch a glimpse of the German pocket battleship *Graf Spee*, one of the raiders known to be at large.

But except for making a brief foray as far as the Mozambique Channel where she sank a British tanker and captured a Norwegian merchantman, the elusive *Graf Spee* preferred to remain to the westward of the Cape of Good Hope. Early in December 1939, she greedily headed for the coast of South America in search of the fat pickings to be found off the River Plate. There she came to an inglorious end by self-immolation after a brusque handling by Commodore Harwood and his squadron of cruisers.

Thus a serious threat was removed from the southern hemisphere, but the *Glorious* was retained in East Indies waters to lend her air squadrons to the prosaic business of trade protection.

In the Mediterranean the uneasy calm continued. The few British warships remaining there were employed in the protection of Allied merchantmen against possible forays by German U-boats, and in operating the contraband control system. Special leniency was however shown to Italian shipping, for there were still hopes that Mussolini could be persuaded to refrain from entering the war.

But early in March 1940, there were hints of Italian troop

movements, the Italian press adopted a more virulent tone towards the Allies, and reports of Italy's warlike intentions were brought to Alexandria by the masters of neutral ships calling at Italian ports. There were also rumours that pressure was being exerted by the Germans on Italy to open the Mediterranean to submarine warfare. At the same time Italian warships became unusually active. Admiral Sir Andrew Cunningham, who had succeeded Pound as Commander-in-Chief, Mediterranean early in 1939, decided to ask for reinforcements.

The *Glorious*, however, was not to return to his command in the Mediterranean. On April 10th the 'phoney war' flared into savage life with the German invasion of Norway. An Allied Expeditionary Force was hastily assembled and despatched to the aid of the hard-pressed Norwegians. But the suddenness of their attack enabled the Germans to capture all the principal airfields, and throughout the campaign the Luftwaffe dominated the skies above Norway.

The *Glorious* was ordered home so that her aircraft, along with those of the *Furious* and their newer and larger sister the *Ark Royal* could provide cover for the Allied landings in Norway until the RAF could improvise airfields from which shore-based aircraft could operate.

British carriers were soon in action. The *Glorious*, now commanded by Captain D'Oyly Hughes – Lyster having been promoted to flag rank – arrived in Norwegian waters with a squadron of RAF Gladiators, whose pilots proceeded to operate from a frozen lake a few miles from Aandalsnes. But these gallant airmen were soon overwhelmed on their novel airfield by enemy bombers.

As other landing grounds were improvised the *Glorious* and *Furious* transported squadrons of RAF Hurricanes and Gladiators from Britain, flying the machines off their decks while still some miles out from the Norwegian coast.

Swordfish aircraft from the *Furious* attacked German warships in Trondheim with torpedoes, while aircraft from the other carriers bombed and strafed targets in the Narvik area. In appalling weather, flying over snow-covered mountains, Fleet Air Arm fighters and torpedo-bombers flew daily sorties against enemy targets, carried out anti-submarine patrols and photographic missions. In spite of the disparity between their own lumbering machines and the high-performance planes of the swarming Luftwaffe they never hesitated to tackle their speedier foes, frequently battling at odds of six to one.

On one occasion an aircraft from the *Glorious* was forced down in a small fjord after being damaged in combat. The pilot and his air gunner swam from their sinking aircraft through icy water to the shore, only to be mistaken for Germans by the Norwegian villagers. After a time they were able to prove their identity, and the Norwegians provided them with food and civilian clothes. Thus disguised, the airmen struggled over seventy miles of mountainous, enemy-infested territory and safely rejoined their ship.

But the Norwegian campaign was doomed to defeat, due chiefly to the lack of air support and our initial failure to secure an adequate base from which to conduct operations. At the beginning of June withdrawal was decided upon. After a brief spell of rest at home, the *Ark Royal* and *Glorious* arrived once more in the Narvik area, the *Ark* to provide air cover for the evacuation, and the *Glorious* to ferry back to Britain the RAF fighters she had so recently transported to Norway.

Due to difficulties of re-embarkation many of the RAF pilots, who had no experience of deck landings, flew their machines on board the *Glorious* rather than leave them behind to be destroyed. All of them landed on safely. But their courage and enterprise was to be in vain.

On June 4th, 1940, a powerful German squadron, which included the battle-cruisers *Scharnhorst* and *Gneisenau*, a heavy cruiser and a number of destroyers, left Kiel with the object of attacking British shipping in northern Norway.

Four days later the *Glorious*, laden with aircraft, stores and flying personnel, was detached from the rest of the British ships at Narvik to return independently to Scapa, escorted by the destroyers *Ardent* and *Acasta*.

Less than three hundred miles from the Norwegian coast the carrier and her escorts were sighted by the German ships. Damaged and set on fire before she could fly off her aircraft, the *Glorious* was speedily sent to the bottom with all but a handful of her company. Soon afterwards her escorts, who had flung themselves gallantly but unavailingly against their massive adversaries, suffered a similar fate.

When the news of the sinking of the *Glorious* filtered through there was grief in the airmen's messes at Hatston, in the Orkneys, at Ford, North Coates and Detling RAF Stations. For at the three last named were Fleet Air Arm squadrons whose crews had formerly served in the *Glorious* under Lyster's command in the Mediterranean at the time of the Munich crisis.

Temporarily grounded at Hatston were the crews of six Swordfish, half of No. 823 Squadron who had been disembarke.. from the *Glorious* before she sailed on what was to be her last voyage. The remainder perished in the carrier. But some of the pilots and observers of these half-dozen aircraft were destined to avenge her loss in the most spectacular Fleet Air Arm feat in history. This day of retribution lay almost exactly five months in the future. But this they could not know.

In the meantime the *Ark Royal* still operating off northern Norway in support of the final stages of the evacuation, despatched a force of fifteen Skuas to exact retribution from the *Scharnhorst*, now tucked away in Trondheim Fjord. Each Skua carried a 500-lb. bomb.

But the distance the aircraft had to fly, and the conditions of almost perpetual daylight in those northern latitudes robbed them of all hope of surprise. The airmen were greeted by a hurricane of ack-ack fire from the battle-cruiser and her escorts, and pounced upon by swarms of enemy fighters who broke up their formation.

Although the vengeful Skua pilots pressed home individual attacks with desperate determination they succeeded in obtaining only one hit on their target, but the bomb failed to explode. Eight of their number failed to return.

This was the last action in the Norwegian campaign.

III

Eight days after the Italian entry into the war, while the two Dictators were clasping hands at Munich and Hitler was pouring his plans for invading the British Isles into Mussolini's avid ear, Winston Churchill, now Prime Minister, informed a shocked House of Commons of the impending final collapse of French resistance. Sparing nothing, he told Parliament and the nation that henceforth Britain stood alone against the Axis Powers.

'Let us therefore brace ourselves to our duties,' he declaimed with heart-stirring oratory, 'and so bear ourselves that if the British Empire and its Commonwealth last for a thousand years men will still say "This was their finest hour".'

Warned of Italian intentions by Mussolini's increasingly bellicose attitude as the Nazi victories continued to mount, the British Admiralty had taken measures to restore the Mediterranean Fleet to its former strength. Four battleships, five cruisers, an aircraft-carrier – the *Eagle*, brought back from the

China Station – several flotillas of destroyers, and a number of submarines now comprised that command. In May Allied naval strength in the Mediterranean was further increased by the addition of a group of French warships.

Later a small but powerful British squadron, destined to achieve fames as 'Force H,' was assembled and based at Gibraltar for the protection of convoy routes to and from West Africa and to operate in the western basin of the Mediterranean.

The defences of Malta were belatedly strengthened against the inevitable Italian attacks now to be expected, although Alexandria had become the new Mediterranean Fleet base; the Red Sea was closed to shipping, and the Suez Canal guarded.

But with the collapse of France the British Admiralty considered the threat posed by the Italians to be so serious that for a time abandonment of the eastern Mediterranean was actually contemplated. Admiral Cunningham fought strenuously against this.

'My men,' he wrote to the First Sea Lord, 'are imbued with a burning desire to get at the Italian fleet.'

IV

On the day that simultaneously brought the news of Italy's entry into the war and the publication of the official communiqué announcing the loss of the *Glorious*, Rear-Admiral Lumley Lyster was on his way back to Britain. He had just closed down the temporary base which had been established at Harstad, a small port on the island of Humoy in Vaags Fjord, of which he had been Flag Officer-in-Charge. It was from this little harbour to the north-east of Narvik that the Allied land assault on that much-battered port had been mounted.

Only a last-minute change of plan had prevented Lyster himself from sailing in the *Glorious*. Thus by a mere quirk of circumstance he was preserved from the fate which overtook his old command.

To his grief at the loss of a fine ship and her gallant company was added a stronger emotion when he learned of the Italian declaration of war. Not only did his country stand in mortal peril from Hitler and his victorious hordes; the Nazi Dictator's 'tattered lackey' – as Churchill was contemptuously to dub Mussolini – had chosen this moment to enter the lists against her.

He recalled those sunlit days of 1938 in Alexandria when, with the highly trained air squadrons of the *Glorious* under his command, a weapon of deadly precision had lain to hand wherewith the fleet and the boastful aspirations of the pompous Duce might have been utterly smashed.

Who now, he wondered, would or could strike the blow at the enemy he detested? The *Glorious* had gone; the *Furious* was now little more than a training carrier; the *Eagle* newly returned from China was too old and slow and her squadrons lacked experience of night flying in the Mediterranean. The *Ark Royal*? She was big and powerful, and her airmen had been blooded in the ill-fated campaign now ended. But she would be needed to spread her air umbrella over the fleet in the coming days of trial in home waters. There was as yet no other carrier ready for service in this swift-moving war, save a new ship called the *Illustrious*. But she was only just out of her building yard.

Yet with Pound, who had first called for the 1938 plan of attack against the Italian fleet, now holding the office of First Sea Lord, and the aggressive Cunningham commanding in the Mediterranean, such an assault would, he felt sure, be made.

Little did he dream in those dark days of June 1940, that he himself would eventually lead it.

CHAPTER III

THE SHIP

ON the bridge of the aircraft-carrier *Illustrious*, creaming through the green seas of the eastern Mediterranean, Captain Denis Boyd squinted at the sky through the binoculars he wore strapped around his neck.

Glistening specks against the cloudless blue above, aircraft whirled and cavorted like mayflies over a summer stream in a dance of death. Italian dive-bombers, spotting the British carrier impudently steaming through the Pantellaria Channel, had swooped to the attack.

But to the surprise of the enemy airmen, who for so long had been accustomed to having things their own way, British fighters rose from her deck to meet them; and the complacency of the Italians fled as they were forced to fling their machines about the sky in an endeavour to evade the deadly lunges of their nimble adversaries.

Boyd grinned appreciatively as he watched the antics of his 'young men', as he called his flyers, and the bridge staff of the fast-steaming carrier grinned with him. The men of the *Illustrious* had known their captain but for a short while, for it was barely four months since the carrier had emerged from her building yard. But that brief and busy period had been time enough for them accurately to sum up their commander as a good man to serve under.

Slimly built and of slightly less than medium height, Captain Denis William Boyd, DSC, was fair-haired and keen-eyed, with a jutting jaw that matched his firm incisive manner.

A torpedo specialist, he had served with distinction in the First World War in submarines and surface craft, earning his decoration for gallantry in the destroyer *Fearless*.

Between the wars he had competently filled a number of staff and technical appointments ashore and afloat, and earned the official commendation of Their Lordships of the Admiralty for his work in perfecting certain improvements to British torpedoes.

Promoted to captain in 1931, Boyd had subsequently served

in command of destroyer flotillas in the Home and Mediterranean Fleets, interrupting this sea time with a spell at the Admiralty as Director of the Tactical Division. His career as a torpedo specialist had finally been crowned by his appointment in 1938 as Captain of H.M.S. *Vernon*, the Navy's torpedo school itself.

Then came the outbreak of the Second World War, and at once the *Vernon* became a vital cog in the naval war machine. Minelaying operations, an intimate concern of this establishment whose scope embraced all forms of underwater warfare, were begun within a few hours of the declaration of war, and a counter-mining department formed to oppose the enemy's efforts.

Trials and experiments with new or improved underwater weapons which had been proceeding at peacetime tempo were speeded up by the pressure of events. Normal training courses for officers and ratings were disrupted and had to be hastily replanned. Air-raid and anti-invasion precautions called for the dispersion to safer areas of certain of the school's technical departments engaged upon secret work.

But busy though he was, Boyd, like most naval officers, ardently desired an active service job afloat. This, he was promised by the Admiralty, would eventually be forthcoming in the shape of command of the new aircraft-carrier *Illustrious*, then building in Messrs. Vickers-Armstrong's yard at Barrow-in-Furness.

That a specialist in underwater warfare should have been selected to command the navy's newest and most modern aircraft-carrier was by no means as strange as it might sound.

Back in 1912 in the early days of naval aviation Boyd had gone to Eastchurch where the Naval Wing of the newly born Royal Flying Corps was centred, and learned to fly an aeroplane 'under the counter', as he phrased it. For, during the birth-pangs of the Royal Naval Air Service, it was not easy for a young junior officer to turn aside from his predestined career to become one of the pioneers of a new arm of unproved value.

Throughout his naval service Boyd kept up his interest in aviation, and flew as often as possible – but as a passenger, since he considered amateur pilots to be a menace! A keen photographer, he had early realised the value of photography in reconnaissance work at sea. While serving as Fleet Torpedo Officer on the staff of the Commander-in-Chief, Mediterranean, in the late 'twenties he had used his own camera to photograph from the air torpedo exercises with the fleet at sea.

At that time, before the advent of radar, naval aviation was still regarded by the fleet as something of a joke. Air reconaissance at sea was largely a hit-or-miss affair, and naval fighters had to be vectored on to a distant enemy by means of smoke shells fired by ships of their own side. But, more often than not, when the fighters eventually reached the point indicated the enemy ships had fled and were nowhere to be seen.

Before the Second World War was many weeks old the Germans began to use the magnetic mine, the first of Hitler's much vaunted 'secret weapons'. For a time while the antidote was being sought in the *Vernon* and elsewhere, the magnetic mine constituted a grave menace to the merchant ships bringing food and raw materials to Britain. One day Boyd was sent for by Winston Churchill, then First Lord of the Admiralty.

'What,' asked Churchill, 'do you know about magnetic mines?'

'Nothing, sir. But I have plenty of officers who do,' replied Boyd uneasily, wondering what was coming.

'Right,' said the First Lord briskly. 'You are to come up to the Admiralty and assist Admiral Wake-Walker, whom I have placed in charge of magnetic mine investigation.'

'But I have been appointed to the *Illustrious*,' protested Boyd, his vision of an important seagoing command collapsing like a house of cards.

'You heard what I said,' growled Churchill, fixing the unhappy captain with a basilisk stare.

Boyd took a deep breath.

'And you heard what I said also, sir,' he retorted.

In the pregnant silence that followed Boyd, appalled at his own temerity, stammered in explanation that the *Illustrious* would not be ready to leave the building yard for another three months, and that he wanted her.

'If we cannot solve the problem of the magnetic mine within three months we never shall,' he ended reasonably.

Churchill nodded thoughtfully.

'I suppose that's true.' Then he added, 'I will see that you get the *Illustrious*.'

And since he knew that Churchill never forgot a promise, Boyd went away comforted.

Towards the end of November 1939, the recovery at Shoeburyness and subsequent stripping down of a German magnetic mine by a team of *Vernon* experts laid bare the secrets of the enemy weapon, and counter-measures were at once put in hand.

The immediate problem had been solved well within the time limit calculated by Boyd. Now he could leave his desk at the Admiralty with a clear conscience and hasten off to sea.

At the end of January 1940, Captain Boyd arrived at Barrow where, in Vickers-Armstrong's yard, he was able to look over his new command.

The *Illustrious*, first of three new aircraft-carriers ordered in 1937, was even larger than the fabulous *Ark Royal*, and a magnificent ship. She was 753 feet long with a waterline beam of 96 feet. Her armoured flight deck – a new and important feature of her construction – extended outboard a further ten feet at either side, and two high-speed lifts gave access to the roomy hangar below. It had been touch and go whether the flight deck and side armour would be forthcoming on schedule. Ordered from the Skoda Works in Czechoslovakia before Hitler's march into that unhappy country, the steel had arrived in Britain only a short time before the Nazi assault on Poland.

The *Illustrious* was armed with sixteen 4.5-inch guns, five multiple pom-poms, seventeen Bofors and twelve Oerlikons. Like the *Ark*, she had an island superstructure on the starboard side of the ship, which contained the navigating bridge, captains' sea cabin, chart room, air intelligence and wireless offices. Her powerful turbines developed 110,000 shaft horsepower which could thrust her great bulk through the water at a top speed of 31 knots.

Since she was an armoured ship she disposed of less hangar space than the *Ark*, which was unarmoured. She therefore carried fewer aircraft: twelve fighters and twenty-four TSR Swordfish. Her total war complement included nineteen hundred officers and men. Altogether a very satisfactory command.

But there was much to be done before the new ship would be ready. At Barrow Boyd met some of the key officers who had been 'standing by' during the building period.

They included the Commander, Gerald Tuck; the gunnery officer, Lieutenant-Commander Herbert Acworth; and the torpedo officer, Lieutenant-Commander Ralph Duckworth, who had previously served with Boyd in destroyers. Commander (E) John Tamplin, a large, fat and happy man, was the senior engineer officer; Lieutenant-Commander Richard Tosswill the navigating officer, an immaculate and quietly spoken individual; 'Rosie' Baker, the First Lieutenant; 'Doc' Keevil, the Surgeon Commander; and Chaplain Henry Lloyd, a former curate from Boyd's brother's parish at Hendon.

The Commander (Flying) was Ian Robertson, known to all as 'Streamline' due to his jutting nose, which gave his aquiline features the look of a ship's prow; and his assistant as Flight Deck Officer was tall, athletic Lieutenant-Commander Douglas ('Haggis') Russell.

It was while Robertson, Tosswill and Acworth were one day animatedly discussing the question of a crest for their new ship during a break in the wardroom that Boyd decided the matter for them.

'When Gideon blew the trumpets the walls of Jericho fell down,' he interposed. 'You three chaps are making so much bloody noise we'll have three trumpets.'

And so it was that three trumpets formed the crest of the new carrier, together with the motto *Vox Non Incerta* – 'no uncertain sound' – thus neatly linking with an appropriate verse from the 14th chapter of St Paul's First Epistle to the Corinthians: 'If the trumpets give an uncertain sound who shall prepare himself to the battle.'

The *Illustrious* formally commissioned for service on April 16th, 1940. Soon after his ship's company arrived Boyd addressed them on the flight deck.

'We commission today one of the finest ships in the navy,' he told them. 'I hope it will be my privilege to bring her into contact with the enemy. What happens then depends upon everyone doing his duty with efficiency and courage. Let us prepare for this test by enthusiasm, zeal and keen understanding. And with a sure faith in the justice of our cause let us place our work and our future in God's hands.'

It was small wonder that under the command of such a man the *Illustrious* was to live up to her name in no uncertain manner.

She had had three predecessors in the last two hundred years. The first, built at Buckler's Hard in 1789, was a 74-gun vessel of some 1,600 tons. This ship fought in two actions against the French in the Mediterranean, and was lost by stranding in 1794.

The second, another 74-gun ship, was launched in 1803, and six years later was present at the attack on the French fleet in the Basque Roads. This was a daring and successful assault upon an enemy fleet in a defended harbour at night, conceived and executed by the brilliant and dashing Lord Cochrane.

The third *Illustrious*, built in 1896 at the height of the Royal Navy's battleship era, was one of a class of nine capital ships. then considered to be the most powerful warships afloat. She played her part in the First World War, but by then she and her

36

sisters had become outdated, and she was sold at the end of that conflict.

Although they could not know it on that chilly day in 1940 at Barrow, the ship's company of the fourth *Illustrious* were to emulate the feat in which the second ship of the name took part, but with very different weapons.

While Boyd was waiting at Barrow for the finishing touches to be put to the new carrier, the Fleet Air Arm squadrons destined to come under his command were earmarked for their floating home. The fighter squadron, equipped with eight Skuas and four of the new 8-gun Fairey Fulmars, was No. 806. The two Swordfish squadrons of twelve aircraft each were Nos. 815 and 819. It is with them that we are chiefly concerned.

First formed in October 1939, No. 815 Squadron was commanded by Lieutenant-Commander Robin Kilroy. After completing their work-up together the squadron was attached to RAF Coastal Command, and had been employed mainly on strikes against enemy shipping, and in minelaying off the Friesian Islands.

With the object to extending the normal endurance range of the Swordfish, Kilroy himself undertook trials with a long-range tank fitted in the after cockpit. Although this meant that no air gunner could be carried, the addition of this extra fuel tank increased the time that the Stringbag could remain in the air by as much as one-and-a-half hours, and so brought the more distant enemy ports and harbours within reach of our mines.

Thus 815 was the first Fleet Air Arm Swordfish squadron to fly with long-range fuel tanks, and their experience in this respect was eventually to prove of great importance.

819 Squadron had formed up at the RN Air Station, Ford, in Sussex, early in 1940. Its nucleus comprised eight pilots from the *Glorious* who had been specially sent home for the purpose while that ship was still operating in the Indian Ocean.

The squadron C.O. was Lieutenant-Commander 'Ginger' Hale, a burly, ruddy-haired individual who played Rugby for England. Cool and imperturbable, Hale was the type of pilot who would fly his Stringbag into the hottest of hot spots with the same single-mindedness and disregard of danger as he would tackle a husky three-quarter on the football field; and his squadron was prepared to follow him to a man.

The rest of the pilots and observers were seasoned flyers, some of whom – like Hale – had served in the *Glorious* back in 1938 when Lyster was in command of the ship. Like their colleagues in 815 Squadron, they were to a large extent hand-picked, and all were experienced in night flying. During the Dunkirk evacuation 819 Squadron, working from an airfield in Kent, flew continuous anti-submarine patrols over the Channel.

The personnel of both squadrons were interviewed by Boyd while the *Illustrious* was completing at Barrow. He told them that the carrier would probably be used to seal off the northern exits from the North Sea with the object of preventing Hitler's heavy ships from breaking through into the Atlantic.

Their aircraft, he said, would almost certainly be required to attack Kiel and Wilhelmshaven. 815 Squadron promptly fashioned a scale model of the latter port in plasticine which they proceeded to study with loving care in between their mine-laying sorties with Coastal Command. Kilroy was not the sort of man to leave anything to chance.

The first few weeks of existence of the newly commissioned carrier were spent on shakedown exercises. But these were of necessity brief, for the war was hotting up with a vengeance. The Norwegian campaign passed into history; Holland, Belgium and France fell under the heel of the invader; Britain herself was threatened with assault; German armed surface raiders ventured forth to aid the ubiquitous U-boats in their efforts to sever our ocean lifelines. No one knew where the next blow would fall.

The *Illustrious* was ordered to embark her air squadrons and sail for Bermuda to carry out working-up exercises. Privately Captain Boyd was informed that as soon as the ship was ready she would be joining Cunningham's command in the Mediterranean. Promotion was also hinted at, for the Mediterranean Fleet included the carrier *Eagle*; as senior captain Boyd would therefore be able to fly his broad pennant as Commodore. Mediterranean Aircraft-Carriers.

But before she left the Clyde workmen and technicians boarded the carrier, and a new and potent device was added to her equipment – radar. With its aid the *Illustrious* would be able to receive warning of approaching aircraft flying as high as 15,000 feet at a distance of sixty miles, and to detect a surface ship at sea nearly seven miles away

With the set came its operator, an enthusiastic Electrical Lieutenant belonging to the Royal Canadian Naval Volunteer Reserve named Schierbeck. The Canadian's loving care of the new device was only matched by his uncanny ability to identify correctly the mysterious blips that appeared on his scan. For this priceless faculty the crew of the *Illustrious* were to be deeply grateful.

On June 11th, 1940, the air squadrons, which had assembled at Roborough, near Plymouth, flew on board the carrier in the Hamoaze. One by one the Fulmars, Skuas and Swordfish landed-on, their touchdown being aided by a batsman – a comparatively new innovation in British aircraft-carriers – and were smartly whisked below to the hangar.

Another innovation was the crash barrier, its purpose to prevent collision with parked aircraft if an arrester wire should break or a tail hook fail to catch. It was the first many of the pilots had ever seen. When the aircrews foregathered later on in the wardroom to compare notes after thoroughly inspecting their new home, they all agreed that the *Illustrious* was a wonderful ship.

It had been intended that the carrier should make Bermuda her temporary base while she cruised about the sunlit waters of the Caribbean, exercising her air squadrons. But on her westward passage, while the German wireless trumpeted the claim that she had been sunk by a U-boat, the *Illustrious* was savagely battered by a stormy Atlantic.

Her degaussing girdle, which consisted of heavy copper strips bolted to the ship's side, was torn away in the buffeting she received. Without this essential protection against enemy magnetic mines the carrier could not be risked at sea. In Bermuda dockyard, therefore, workmen laboured mightily under the direction of Duckworth, the torpedo officer, to make good the damage.

But this severely curtailed the programme of flying training. Day exercises had to be carried out at anchor. Nevertheless flying went on continuously, particularly for the Swordfish squadrons. 'Streamline' Robertson was a perfectionist, and accordingly he was freely cursed by the aircrews. But their moans were without resentment, for his personal charm was almost as potent as that of Captain Boyd. And there was little one could tell Robertson about flying the Fairey Swordfish, for he had commanded the very first Fleet Air Arm squadron to be equipped with them on board the *Glorious* in August 1936.

On July 23rd the *Illustrious* arrived back in the Clyde, ship's company and aircrews well on the way to becoming a close-knit team. The fighters and bombers were flown off to Abbotsinch, from which air station their crews were able to snatch a few days' leave.

On August 11th the airmen re-embarked, No. 806 Squadron

having in the meantime been completely equipped with Fulmars, and the ship prepared for sea. A week later Boyd was considerably jolted when Rear-Admiral Lumley Lyster arrived on board and hoisted his flag as Rear-Admiral, Aircraft-Carriers, Mediterranean.

Boyd had known of Lyster as a Service colleague of note for more than twenty years, but until August 19th, 1940, when the latter stepped on board the two men had never met personally long enough to shake hands.

Swallowing his natural disappointment at his relegation to the post of mere Chief Staff Officer to the Senior Officer of the Mediterranean Aircraft-Carriers instead of exercising that command himself, Boyd accepted the position philosophically and prepared to work loyally with his admiral. He soon formed a great admiration for the tough, aggressive flag officer, who lost no time in planning ways and means of annoying the enemy.

For his part, Admiral Lyster was almost equally surprised, and certainly delighted, to find himself on board the *Illustrious*. After his return from Norway he had been given the appointment of Flag Officer in Charge of the Orkneys, and had contemplated with some distaste a lengthy stay in this gloomy northern outpost. Determined to extract what comfort he could from the situation, he had sent for his wife and daughters to join him. Only too happy to be with her husband, Daisy Lyster had closed up their house in Dorset and hastened north with one of the girls; Beryl the second daughter had joined the Wrens. But scarcely had Mrs Lyster arrived than the admiral packed his bags and departed.

Three days after Lyster's flag had been hoisted the *Illustrious*, in company with the battleship *Valiant*, the anti-aircraft ships *Calcutta* and *Coventry* and a large convoy, sailed for Gibraltar and the Mediterranean.

II

Meanwhile Admiral Cunningham was gratified to learn that, in part at least, his requests for reinforcements were about to be met, and that the additions to his fleet were to include an aircraft-carrier with an armoured deck. For air power was soon to become a vital factor in the Mediterranean.

With the French fleet out of the fight Italy dominated that sea, with Sicily at her foot narrowing still further the channel between the enemy mainland and North Africa. To east and west stretched hostile coastlines, with Gibraltar itself in jeopardy if Hitler could make a deal with Franco.

Although the Italian fleet seemed reluctant to emerge from its harbours, the Regia Aeronautica was busy spying on Cunningham's every move. Each time the British fleet put to sea from Alexandria the inevitable Italian shadower from Rhodes appeared in the sky, to be followed by enemy bombers who had been homed on to their comrade. Without a proper fighter squadron there was little the *Eagle* could do about it. But now that situation was to be remedied.

The *Illustrious* and her consorts reached Gibraltar on August 29th, and next day sailed to join Admiral Cunningham, who planned to meet the newcomers to his flag at a rendezvous to the south of Sicily. The opportunity was also taken to convey stores and provisions to Malta and in the eastbound warship to Alexandria. The *Illustrious* herself was crammed with supplies for the fleet, which included ammunition, mines, guns and petrol, odd corners of the hangar even being pressed into service for the stowage of these vital necessities. The whole operation was given the code name 'HATS', standing for 'Hands Across the Sea'.

Off Sardinia, Force H, which had been escorting them, parted company to swing northwards and harry the enemy, while the *Illustrious*, *Valiant* and the two AA cruisers pressed on through the Pantellaria Channel. The ships passed so close to the island itself during the hours of darkness that lookouts aboard the *Illustrious* swore they could see the flare of matches ashore as the Italian sentries lit their cigarettes.

On the morning of September 2nd Cunningham's ships were sighted. The junction was effected by 9 a.m., and the fleet turned about for Alexandria. On the previous day a patrolling Swordfish from the *Eagle* had spotted the Italian battlefleet at sea, but once again the enemy retreated without attempting to attack.

Nevertheless Italian shore-based aircraft raced out to pounce on the *Illustrious*. Their bombs all fell wide, and then suddenly the British naval fighters got among the Italian airmen. Three of the bombers were sent reeling out of the sky as a result of this encounter; the rest fled, and Boyd and Lyster were well satisfied.

But the *Illustrious* intended to play herself in for her long and successful Mediterranean innings with a further aggressive display.

Escorted by destroyers, and with her elderly sister the *Eagle* in company, the carrier turned away to the north-east and headed for the island of Rhodes, from whose airfields Italian airmen had long plagued Cunningham's ships at Alexandria.

At a quarter to four in the morning of September 4th, eight Swordfish from 815 and 819 Squadrons rose into the darkness from the flight deck of the *Illustrious* and viciously plastered the aerodrome at Calato with bombs, starting fires in the enemy hangars and amid their parked aircraft.

Fifteen minutes later Swordfish of 813 and 824 Squadrons from the *Eagle* swooped down upon Martiza airfield with equally unpleasant results to the enemy. The Stringbags landed back on their respective carriers without mishap, and the ships sped southward to rejoin Admiral Cunningham.

Later that morning the enraged Italians struck back with their bombers at the retiring British, but without success, and the augmented Mediterranean Fleet safely re-entered Alexandria.

As soon as the ships had secured to their moorings Admiral Lyster hastened over to the fleet flagship to wait upon his Commander-in-Chief in accordance with custom. After a discussion on the situation in the Mediterranean, during which Cunningham outlined the difficulties with which he was faced, Lyster brought up the subject of a naval air attack upon the enemy fleet. He recalled the plan he had prepared in 1938 and suggested that this should be revived and held in readiness to be put into operation at an opportune moment. Cunningham listened attentively and his reception of the proposal was not discouraging.

But as yet these were early days. The quality of Mussolini's Navy had still to be tested, while on land there were indications that the Italians were preparing to invade Egypt. There would be much for the airmen of the *Illustrious* to do besides the intensive exercises needed to fit them to make such an attack. Nevertheless Lyster was told that he could go ahead with the development of his plan.

On September 13th, 1940, Marshal Graziani began this slow advance over the Egyptian border. Two days later Swordfish from the *Illustrious* took off to dive-bomb the harbour at Benghazi and lay mines in its approaches.

819 Squadron was disembarked to Dekheila in order to be able to work more closely with the British Army of the Nile. 815 Squadron kept up the good work along the coast, sinking two Italian supply ships at Benghazi, while a third enemy vessel

was destroyed after striking one of the mines laid by the String-bags.

In the meantime a squadron of twin-engined Italian bombers based on Rhodes, calling themselves 'The Green Mice', made the *Illustrious* their special quarry. But since the big carrier was able to detect the approach of enemy aircraft with her radar 'The Green Mice' met with some brusque handling in their attacks.

Whenever they were not actively engaged in harassing the Italian land forces and their supply ships the aircrews of the torpedo-bombers of both carriers were exercised in the special technique that would be required for a successful assault upon an enemy fleet in its own defended harbour.

As soon as the *Illustrious* sailed for the Mediterranean, Lyster had set his Staff Officer (Operations), Commander Charles Thompson, and the latter's assistant, Lieutenant David Pollock, RNVR, to work on drafting a fresh plan of attack on Taranto. The CO of 815 Squadron, now Lieutenant-Commander Kenneth Williamson, who had relieved Kilroy shortly before the carrier's departure from the United Kingdom, and Hale, commanding 819 Squadron, had been consulted and had given their views. But as yet the plan still remained tentative, for there were many changed factors to be taken into consideration.

As time wore on, however, Lyster's impatience manifested itself in a letter he sent to the Commander-in-Chief.

'They (the Italians) show no inclination to venture far from the gulf of Taranto,' he wrote, 'and since it is not easy to find any inducement to make them do so, air attack on the harbour must be considered.'

Admiral Cunningham agreed, for he was in fact considering precisely that alternative to his dwindling hope of meeting and destroying the Italian main fleet in a ship-to-ship surface action.

CHAPTER IV

OPERATION JUDGEMENT

AT dawn on June 11th, 1940, the day following Mussolini's declaration of war, a powerful force of French and British warships sailed from Alexandria. Once out of sight of land the fleet split up. The French squadron of cruisers and destroyers turned eastwards towards the Aegean. The British force, comprising two battleships, five cruisers, the aircraft-carrier *Eagle*, and escorting destroyers, steamed westward.

Systematically the two fleets swept the whole vast area of the eastern and central Mediterranean, the British ships closing almost to within gun range of southern Italy. But not a single unit of Mussolini's fleet was sighted. On their way back to Alexandria two of the British cruisers shelled a group of Italian minesweepers off Tobruk. Admiral Sir Andrew Cunningham, British naval Commander-in-Chief in the Mediterranean, had lost no time in seeking to bring the new enemy to battle.

Two weeks later came the collapse of France. The French Navy was out of the fight, and their eastern squadron lay demilitarised at Alexandria. The balance of naval power in the Mediterranean had now swung decisively in favour of Italy.

On that grim day when Britain found herself fighting alone against the Axis, Admiral Cunningham summoned his captains to his flagship, the battleship *Warspite*, at Alexandria. The situation appeared to be so desperate that some of them were quite convinced that they were about to be ordered to withdraw their ships from the Mediterranean altogether. Instead the Commander-in-Chief calmly told them, 'Gentlemen, I have called you together to discuss how best we can annoy the enemy.' His policy, he made it abundantly clear, was to be one of aggressiveness.

Admiral Sir Andrew Cunningham was the right man in the right place at the right time. He had passed the greater part of his naval career in destroyers, and since it is not uncommon for these small ships to find themselves pitted against adversaries considerably larger than themselves he, like all destroyer commanders, was used to facing odds. In addition, his knowledge and experience of the Mediterranean were probably unique.

He had commanded a destroyer in the Mediterranean for a large part of the First World War. Later as a rear-admiral in the early 'thirties he had commanded the Mediterranean destroyer flotillas. In 1937 he became Second-in-Command of the Mediterranean Fleet. For twelve months prior to the outbreak of the Second World War he had held the post of Deputy Chief of the Naval Staff at the Admiralty before going out to the Mediterranean yet again, this time as Commander-in-Chief.

In addition to their principal task of supplying Malta and maintaining the flow of shipping in the eastern Mediterranean, Cunningham's ships continued to sally forth on periodical sweeps in search of the enemy. But, except for the destruction of one Italian destroyer and three submarines on different occasions, they all proved abortive. He sighted the Italian battle-fleet only once.

The encounter took place early in July when two important convoys were being sailed from Malta, carrying women and children, who had been evacuated from the island, and stores to Alexandria. In order to meet and protect these two convoys Admiral Cunningham put to sea with almost all of his available ships.

For the purpose of the operation he split his fleet into three groups. He himself, with his flag in the battleship *Warspite*, was accompanied by five destroyers. Vice-Admiral Tovey, his second-in-command, was in the cruiser *Orion*, and with him were four other cruisers and an Australian destroyer. The third and largest force comprised the battleships *Royal Sovereign* and *Malaya*, the aircraft-carrier *Eagle*, and a destroyer screen. In command was Rear-Admiral Pridham-Wippell. On July 7th the ships left Alexandria and headed north-westward.

But the usual Italian shadowing aircraft had seen and reported their departure. On the following day enemy bombers from bases in the Dodecanese came out to attack them in waves. For more than six hours from noon onwards, with no protecting fighters overhead, the British warships had to endure seven determined air assaults. Fifty heavy bombs were hurled at the *Warspite* alone, but they all missed. Tovey's and Pridham-Wippell's forces were equally heavily attacked, but only one cruiser, the *Gloucester*, was hit. The bomb which struck her killed eighteen officers and men, among them the cruiser's captain.

During the afternoon while Cunningham's ships were dodging and swerving under the lash of these attacks, an RAF

Sunderland flying boat on patrol reported sighting a powerful enemy fleet of three battleships, six cruisers and seven destroyers steaming northwards from Benghazi. The Italians were obviously on their way home after completing one of their own convoy operations. Cunningham immediately cracked on speed with the intention of cutting off the enemy from their base in Italy.

On the following day the two fleets were only ninety miles apart. The enemy force was now known to consist of two battleships, instead of the three originally reported, twelve cruisers and a score of destroyers. Swordfish aircraft from the *Eagle* were sent off in waves to try to cripple the larger enemy units, but the airmen only managed to score one hit on a cruiser.

Although the Italians were now almost within the shadow of their own coast Cunningham pressed on in pursuit. But Campioni, the Italian admiral, had no real stomach for a fight and, after the *Cesare*, one of his battleships, had been hit by a fifteen-inch shell fired by the *Warspite* at extreme range, he put up a smoke screen and fled for home.

Cunningham continued the chase until the Calabrian coast was actually in sight and shore-based enemy bombers came racing out to the attack. Then, when it was clear that the Italian ships could not be brought to battle, the British fleet turned southwards for Malta to refuel. Despite the constant bombing attacks they had to endure all the way back to Alexandria with the convoys, none of the British ships other than the *Gloucester* which had been hit earlier on suffered any damage.

This disappointing brush off Calabria seemed to have set the pattern of the naval war in the Mediterranean, for on two subsequent occasions the Italian fleet found itself in the vicinity of the British fleet, once in superior numbers. But on both occasions the Italians avoided action.

Nevertheless Cunningham kept up the pressure. The Italian lines of communication to their bases in the Dodecanese were particularly vulnerable. British light forces made continual sorties to attack these routes and met with some minor successes.

In the meantime, however, the enemy was building up his land forces in Libya and this was more difficult to prevent. Tripoli is little more than a night's fast steaming from Sicily, while Alexandria is nearly a thousand miles away. The few British submarines which for a time were able to work from Malta did what they could to interrupt the enemy convoys, but conditions were against them and they never became a serious threat. Nor could heavily bombed Malta be used as a base from which light surface forces could operate. Reconnaissance aircraft from Rhodes and Leros kept a close watch on Cunningham's fleet in the eastern Mediterranean, and this constant surveillance enabled the Italians to choose safe periods during which to run their convoys as far eastward as Benghazi.

As Marshal Graziani's forces were steadily strengthened and the land threat to Egypt grew daily more menacing, the Mediterranean Fleet used its guns to harass the Italians along their seaward flank. Battleships and cruisers shelled Bardia, destroyers and gunboats bombarded other harbours and troop concentrations, and Swordfish aircraft from the *Eagle* swooped down on enemy supply ships.

Malta, too, had to be constantly nourished and sustained. But each convoy to the beleaguered island constituted a major operation for Admiral Cunningham, since always and exasperatingly, there loomed in the background the latent threat of the Italian battle fleet in being. The possibility that the enemy ships might emerge at some inconvenient moment prevented him from deploying his forces as he wished.

To meet his growing commitments Cunningham had asked for reinforcements, and in August he learned that these were on the way in the shape of the battleship *Valiant*, the new aircraft-carrier *Illustrious*, and two anti-aircraft cruisers. If the Italians would not come out and fight he must employ other tactics. The arrival of the *Illustrious* gave him the means to do so.

Then came the Italian invasion of Egypt on September 13th, and bombardments from the sea had to be stepped up to delay the advancing enemy. Swordfish aircraft from the *Eagle* and *Illustrious* mined Tobruk and torpedoed enemy supply ships in Benghazi. But once he reached Sidi Barrani, Graziani unaccountably paused and began to dig himself in.

During this lull in the land campaign Admiral Cunningham turned once more to the problem of the Italian fleet, and considered Lyster's plan for attacking the ships in their own harbour. But apart from the intensive training needed by the Swordfish crews to fit them for such an enterprise, one essential requirement was adequate reconnaissance of the enemy's main base of Taranto.

Until early in September RAF Sunderland flying boats had been the only aircraft available for reconnaissance work, and they were quite unsuitable for this particular task. But within a week of the *Illustrious* joining the Mediterranean Fleet a number of American built, high-speed, long-range RAF aircraft had arrived in Malta to take over reconnaissance duties. Accordingly they were instructed to commence a regular watch on Taranto.

By mid-October the Commander-in-Chief was informed by Admiral Lyster that the aircrews of the carriers were ready to carry out the operation. Reconnaissance photographs of Taranto had been obtained by the RAF's new Maryland aircraft from Malta showing the location in the harbour of the enemy's major units. The plan of attack was thereupon finalised to take place on the night of October 21st.

In essence the plan was similar to that originally drafted by Willoughby and Mackintosh on board the *Glorious* in September 1938: a moonlight torpedo attack against battleships and cruisers in Taranto's outer harbour combined with diversionary bombing attacks against the smaller ships in the inner harbour.

Thirty Swordfish were to take part, attacking in two waves of fifteen aircraft each. Nine Swordfish in each range would carry torpedoes and six would act as dive-bombers. The carriers were to be in such a position that the aircraft would not be required to fly more than four hundred miles to and from the target.

As Trafalgar Day approached the work of preparing the aircraft for the operation began to go ahead. One morning on board the *Illustrious* the brightly lit hangar was humming with activity. Fitters and riggers swarmed over the squatting Swordfish testing engines and checking over airframes and rigging. Air gunners were fitting the overload tanks in position.

Presently one of the gunners straightened up from his task for a brief respite. As he did so his foot slipped on the greasy floor of the Stringbag's cockpit. He lost his balance, clutched wildly at the empty air, then fell heavily. The screwdriver with which he had been securing the metal strap of the tank struck a pair of exposed terminals in the cockpit, which immediately sparked.

The atmosphere in that enclosed space was saturated with petrol fumes. Instantly the spark touched off a flash, the flash an explosion. The whole tail section of the aircraft disintegrated. As the gunner was blown clear the Stringbag burst into flames. Other aircraft nearby were were swiftly engulfed.

The whole thing had happened in little more than a split second, and at once the crowded hangar – and the ship herself – were in dire peril. But the drill for just such an emergency had been constantly practised. Fire fighting parties snapped into action; the spray extinguishers were switched on. In a matter of minutes the fire had been put out, and the extent of its ravages was being anxiously assessed.

Two Swordfish were probable write-offs, others only slightly damaged. But all the rest were swamped with salt water from the extinguishers. Not one machine out of the two squadrons was fit to fly.

There was no point in blaming the individual whose unfortunate slip had brought about the calamity. It was a sheer accident, and it might have had even more devastating results. But the occurrence emphasised to a frightening degree upon what slender thread of chance hung the whole fate of the British fleet in the Mediterranean, perhaps even the course of the war itself.

Boyd sent an official report of the fire to Admiral Lyster, and Lyster passed the report on to the Commander-in-Chief. The great attack would have to be postponed.

Every one of the Swordfish in the *Illustrious*, other than the two which had been irreparably damaged by the fire, had to be taken up to the flight deck and thoroughly washed out with fresh water. The engines had to be completely stripped down, and all the instruments, including the wireless sets, taken to pieces, dried, cleaned and reassembled. The work took many hours, even with all hands labouring unceasingly night and day.

But at last the job was finished and the Swordfish were once more ready to fly. Now another date had to be chosen which would allow the crews time for rehearsal, and for the correction of any defects which might manifest themselves in the aircraft after their recent ordeal.

A week later, however, Admiral Cunningham was faced with a fresh and more serious situation. At three o'clock on the morning of October 28th the Italians delivered an ultimatum to Greece demanding the occupation of certain key points in that country. These demands were indignantly rejected, but even before the ultimatum expired Italian ground forces crossed the Albanian border into Greece, and Italian aircraft raided Patras, Corinth and Athens itself. The Greek Government immediately appealed to Britain for aid.

Once more we had an ally in the Mediterranean, but the Greek Navy was small, and Admiral Cunningham knew that the main task of defending her coasts and islands against the enemy would fall on his already overburdened ships.

The first necessity was the establishment of an advanced

fuelling base at Suda Bay, in Crete, which would thereafter require to be supplied and defended. The despatch of troops and stores to Greece would also involve him in fresh problems of transport and convoy protection against attacks from the enemy bases in the Dodecanese.

The air assault on Taranto had been postponed until the night of October 30-31st. On that day the Commander-in-Chief was cruising to the westward of Crete with the battle fleet, covering the passage of a convoy of tankers en route for Suda Bay. However there was no moon that night, and since the air-crews had not been trained in the use of flares which would be necessary to light up the targets, the assault had to be further postponed.

The situation in the Middle East was now rapidly becoming critical. The Italians were advancing in Greece and Libya, and our garrisons in East Africa and the Sudan were menaced by powerful Italian armies. It was essential to remove the threat posed by the Italian fleet once and for all.

The next convenient date for the air blow against Taranto had been fixed by the planning staffs as November 11th. Alternative dates when the moon would serve were November 17th, 18th and 19th. In the same way as Trafalgar Day had been considered psychologically appropriate for the attack on Taranto, November 11th was also a significant date. Twenty-two years earlier it had heralded a cease-fire at the plea of a vanquished foe. November 11th, 1940, might well usher in the beginning of the end for another enemy. But there were certain more cogent reasons which decided the Commander-in-Chief to choose that particular date.

As a result of Mussolini's unprovoked attack on Greece, measures had been taken at home to reinforce Admiral Cunningham's fleet still further. On their way out from England at the beginning of November, therefore, were another battleship, the *Barham*; two cruisers, the *Berwick* and *Glasgow*, and some additional destroyers. These warships were also carrying on board two thousand troop reinforcements and a number of badly needed guns for the garrison of Malta.

In the eastern Mediterranean various shipping movements were impending. A fully laden convoy for Malta was assembled at Alexandria, while in Malta a number of merchantmen in ballast awaited onward transit to Egypt. Troops, stores and fuel were due to be transported to the new base at Suda Bay, and personnel and fuel for the RAF bombers in Greece needed to be conveyed to the Piraeus. These convoying activities and the arrival in the Mediterranean of the reinforcing warships which were to join his flag were all scheduled to take place between November 4th and November 12th.

Admiral Cunningham accordingly drew up an overall plan to cover the whole of these complex movements, which was given the title of 'Operation MB8'.

The safe arrival in Malta of the additional troops which had been despatched from the United Kingdom was absolutely essential. The passage of the warships in which they were embarked from Gibraltar to the central Mediterranean would therefore be covered by Admiral Somerville's Force H. This part of Plan MB8 was code-named 'Operation Coat'.

Somerville was flying his flag in the aircraft-carrier *Ark Royal*, and he had with him the cruiser *Sheffield* and eight destroyers. He therefore ordered three of the destroyers to join up with the *Barham* and her consorts for the voyage to Malta. With the rest of Force H he would remain within striking distance of the troop-carrying ships until they reached a point 160 miles west of Sicily where they would be transferred to Cunningham's protection. En route aircraft from the *Ark Royal* would take off and bomb Cagliari in a subsidiary operation to be known as 'Crack'.

The convoy at Alexandria which was destined for Malta comprised five supply ships, three of them carrying cased petrol. Cunningham routed this convoy north of Crete, and with it he decided to send as far as Suda Bay two more merchantmen carrying anti-aircraft guns, motor transport, fuel and petrol which were urgently required for the establishment of that base. From Malta the four empty merchantmen awaiting passage would be taken back to Egypt by the escorts of the inward bound convoy.

The first ships to move would be three vessels laden with fuel and petrol for Greece, which were due to leave Alexandria accompanied by a small escort on November 4th.

In addition to the sailings of these merchant-ship convoys the Commander-in-Chief also decided to send extra troops and equipment from Port Said to Suda Bay in the cruisers *Ajax* and *Sydney*, and to transport to Greece in the cruiser *Orion* the stores and personnel which were required by the RAF. Vice-Admiral Pridham-Wippell, who commanded the light forces, was flying his flag in the latter vessel. After calling at the Piraeus, where he would confer with the Greek authorities, he was to continue on and examine the situation in Crete.

When the first of these moves had begun with the departure of the Greek convoy from Alexandria, Admiral Cunningham planned to sail himself on November 6th with the battle fleet and his aircraft-carriers to take up a central position from which he could deal with any threat of interference by the Italians, and link up with the reinforcements coming to him from Gibraltar.

The Commander-in-Chief now fitted into Plan MB8 the air strike against Taranto on the 11th, to which he gave the appropriate code name of 'Operation Judgment'.

Finally, with the object of enheartening the Greeks, he added a raid by Pridham-Wippell's light forces into the Straits of Otranto to take place on that same night, where he hoped they might be able to pounce upon the regular convoy the enemy was in the habit of running across the Adriatic after dark.

But when all was ready for this vast and complex plan to slip into gear, Captain Bridge of the *Eagle* was reluctantly compelled to report to the Commander-in-Chief a discovery which threatened yet again to wreck Operation Judgment. The savage enemy bombing which the old carrier had endured back in July had caused serious defects to develop in her petrol system. It was impossible for these to be temporarily patched up; nothing short of a major overhaul in the dockyard was required. She would therefore be unable to sail with the fleet as planned.

Admiral Cunningham had grown inured to this sort of disappointment. In any case matters were too far advanced to cancel or drastically alter any part of MB8. He decided that the operation should proceed as planned with one carrier only. But to make up the number of aircraft required for Operation Judgment, the *Eagle* was ordered to transfer to her consort five of her Swordfish and eight complete crews.

Meanwhile certain amendments were found necessary to the scheme of attack on Taranto. The number of aircraft now available, even including the reinforcements from the *Eagle*, reduced the striking force from thirty to twenty-four. This would permit of two waves of twelve aircraft each. Since the obstructions caused by the enemy net and other defences restricted the number of suitable torpedo-dropping positions, only six aircraft in each strike would be armed with torpedoes.

Also, as the direction of the moon would have altered, flares would have to be used. Lastly, in order to lessen the risk of meeting enemy surface craft leaving the Taranto gulf or the

Otranto Straits after dark, the operation would be carried out earlier in the night than had been originally arranged in October.

The final plan for the Judgment operation as drawn up by Lyster and Boyd and approved by the Commander-in-Chief, then, was for the *Illustrious* and her escorting ships to be detached from the main fleet early in the evening of November 11th. By eight o'clock the carrier was to reach a position some forty miles due west of Kabbo Point, the most westerly promontory in the Greek island of Cephalonia. From this position, known as 'X for X-ray,' she would launch the first strike of Swordfish, which would then have 170 miles to fly to Taranto. One hour later the second strike would be flown off from the same position.

Thus the first attack was due to hit Taranto shortly before 10 p.m., and the second at about fifteen minutes to midnight.

Both waves were to fly up the centre of the Gulf of Taranto and approach the enemy base from the south-west. The primary torpedo attack was to be preceded by aircraft dropping flares, and dive-bombing attacks on the enemy cruisers and destroyers.

In the meantime the carrier force would steam up and down in the vicinity of Cephalonia. They would then return to a second position, known as 'Y for Yorker,' twenty miles from the island, by one o'clock in the morning of the 12th, ready for the *Illustrious* to land on the returning aircraft.

Adequate reconnaissance over Taranto must continue to be flown by the RAF, and arrangements would be made for last-minute photographs of the base to be collected from Malta by an aircraft from the *Illustrious* on the morning of D-Day.

Thus finally the scene was set for what all concerned hoped would prove to be the greatest and most successful achievement in the history of naval aviation.

CHAPTER V

WATCH ON TARANTO

ON the night of September 6th, 1940, just one week after the
Illustrious had arrived in the Mediterranean, three twin-engined
aircraft roared off the runway of the RAF Station at Thorney
Island. Climbing rapidly, they turned on to a south-easterly
course and vanished into the darkening sky. They were due to
arrive in Malta at dawn the next day.

To the eyes of any but an expert in aircraft recognition the
planes showed unfamiliar outlines, for only a few of them
had been seen in Britain, engaged in brief training flights over
the eastern counties. Although they bore RAF markings, they
had in fact been designed and built in America.

From the assembly shops of the Glenn Martin Aircraft
Company, of Baltimore in the State of Maryland, where they
had recently taken shape, the planes had been crated and shipped
across the Atlantic consigned to the French Air Force. They
formed the residue of a contract which had been placed in
America by the French Air Ministry several months earlier for
a new type of long-range bomber-reconnaissance aircraft.

But before delivery could be completed the Nazi blitzkrieg
had shattered the French armies and rolled up the British
Expeditionary Force. From Bordeaux a new government of
France headed by Marshal Petain and the treacherous Laval
sued for an armistice with the victorious Hitler.

Accordingly the valuable crates were hastily diverted to
Britain where the RAF took over and assembled their contents,
named them 'Marylands', and modified and adapted their
equipment to meet British requirements. Priceless additions to
the RAF's meagre force of photographic reconnaissance aircraft, three of them were being dispatched to the Mediterranean
to make good grievous deficiencies in this important component
of our our Middle East air strength.

Since the outbreak of war it had rapidly become apparent
that air reconnaissance by medium-performance machines, such
as had been carried out in the First World War, was no longer
practicable. In order to be able to penetrate into well-defended

54

enemy territory and operate successfully against radar and fast fighter planes, aircraft were required which combined high speed with long range. At home a handful of Spitfires had been converted for the job, but there were few of these to spare. The Glenn Martin 'Maryland' therefore filled the bill admirably.

As the trio of American-built planes headed out over the Channel in tight formation, Luftwaffe bombers were preparing to take off from airfields in France and Holland for their nightly attacks on this country. Soon they would fill the skies over England with their sinister drone by day as well as by night, for the Battle of Britain was about to begin. Thus the three Marylands were merely exchanging one embattled island for another.

In the pilot's seat of the leading machine sat Squadron Leader Ernest Alfred Whitely. Small and fair-haired, Whiteley possessed all the essential qualities of leadership. He was tough, enterprising and courageous, and an experienced and capable pilot. Until a few days previously he had been serving with No. 22 Beaufort (Torpedo) Squadron of RAF Coastal Command, based at North Coates, in Lincolnshire.

Then at the beginning of September Whiteley was sent for and informed that he had been selected to take over command of a new unit which was about to be formed as No. 431 General Reconnaissance Flight and sent to Malta as soon as possible. The unit would be equipped with three Marylands at first, he was told. Later, if he was lucky, he might get three more.

Since there seemed to be some degree of urgency about the matter Whiteley did not wait to receive written confirmation of these orders. With Pilot Officer Foxton and Flight Sergeant Bibby, the two other pilots from No. 22 Squadron who had been assigned to him, he promptly began a conversion course on the Marylands.

For the direct flight to Malta across France, night-flying experience on the American planes and an understanding of the icing problems were essential. During the first few days of September, therefore, the three pilots got in as many flying hours in their new machines as possible. But the constant air activity over Britain at that time seriously hampered their vitally necessary night-flying training.

The first time that Whiteley himself went up for night-landing practice he was taken for a Hun and fired on by the gunners at every airfield at which he tried to land. Eventually he had to give up in disgust and, to pass away the hours until dawn, he flew to Holland and back three times. At daybreak he touched down at North Coates without having achieved a single night landing! He was furious about this, but no one could be blamed. It was just another hazard to be added to the rest of their difficulties.

The official intention had been that the unit should be formed up on September 19th, and proceed to Malta as soon after that date as possible. Unaware of this, however, Whiteley and his men, having satisfactorily mastered the intricacies of their new machines, duly set off for Malta on September 6th.

They flew through the night over occupied and unoccupied France without incident, and exercised their new function by photographing certain interesting portions of Sardinia as they passed over that island at dawn. Two hours later the patch-work terrain of Malta loomed up below. The Marylands circled briefly, then came in smoothly to land on Luca airfield under the curious gaze of a small group of Hurricane pilots who happened at that moment to be resting between patrols.

As Whiteley and his men walked over to report to Air Commodore Jonas, the station commander, they noticed all round the airfield signs of the daily visitations by enemy bombers which from now on would become part of their lot.

Ever since Mussolini's entry into the war the Italian air force had gone all out to smash the island's resistance. But to the pained surprise of the Regia Aeronautica the Maltese stubbornly refused to give in.

At the outset of hostilities with Italy there were no fighter planes in Malta, merely a few obsolete London flying boats. But four crated Gloster Gladiators had been left in store at Malta by the aircraft-carrier *Glorious*. The flying boat pilots uncrated these superannuated biplanes, learned to fly them and, after one had been shot down, with the three that remained – nicknamed Faith, Hope and Charity – continued to engage in combat with the whole Italian air force. Since then a squadron of Hurricanes had been flown in to take over the air defence of the island.

But the long drawn-out agony of Malta was only just beginning.

Feeding the overcrowded population and supplying the garrison became an almost insuperable problem. Malta was compelled to depend upon the navy to bring in the vitally needed supplies of arms, equipment, fuel, petrol and food. Every time that a convoy was successfully fought through, the Maltese thronged the terraces overlooking the waterfront and cheered themselves hoarse as the bomb-scarred ships limped into the Grand Harbour.

There were only four airfields within the island's 117 square miles. These were Luca, a short distance south of Valetta, the capital; Ta Kali to the north-west; and Hal Far and the old seaplane base of Calafrana to the south-east. All four were gallantly defended by men of the Royal Artillery and the Royal Malta Artillery.

This, then, was the Malta in which Whiteley, his aircrews and their small ground staff found themselves. A beleaguered island of incessantly shrieking sirens and exploding bombs, of hardship and privation, and the daily threat of annihilation. But these conditions had to be endured, for there was a job of work to be done and Malta was the best place from which to do it.

The task of 431 Flight, Whiteley was informed, was to photograph harbours and aerodromes in Sicily and Italy as far north as Naples and eastward to Brindisi; to search the sea for enemy shipping between Malta, Tunis and Tripoli; and maintain constant surveillance over a sizeable chunk of the Ionian Sea.

The whole area formed a vast corridor through which Mussolini could send his warships and convoys to North Africa, lie in wait to disrupt the Royal Navy's tenuous line of communication between Gibraltar and Alexandria, and attack Malta itself. It was just about the most important sector in the whole Mediterranean theatre of war.

In addition the navy wanted daily cover and detailed reconnaissance of heavily defended enemy naval bases, such as Taranto. Sunderland flying boats of RAF Middle East Command had been doing sterling work, but they were too slow and vulnerable. Speedier and more manoeuvrable aircraft were required for the job.

The Marylands would be a godsend. With a top speed of 270 miles an hour, they could hurtle in over an enemy base, probe its defences, and be off out of reach before the Italian fighters could get into the air.

Nevertheless Whiteley knew that the job was going to be difficult and hazardous. There were endless worries ahead. His aircraft might be put out of action by bombs while on the ground; they might be shot up in the air; or – and this was his biggest headache – become unserviceable due to lack of spares, for of these there were virtually none.

He ordered the ground staff to keep the planes as widely

dispersed as possible at all times while they were on the airfield in order to minimise the risk of damage by bombing or strafing. He warned his pilots not to take unnecessary risks in the air, and especially to resist the impulse to shoot-up tempting targets. Their job was to bring back pictures, not to engage in air battles. The four guns in the Maryland were promising weapons but they were strictly for defensive purposes only.

But Whiteley's greatest need was for more aircraft. Before he left England he had been promised three additional Marylands. In the event only one arrived. He pleaded for others, but was curtly told that none could be spared. Instead he was grudgingly loaned two Blenheim Mark IV's and a Naval Skua, whose performance was far below that of the US-built planes. The latter had therefore to be kept for the more difficult operations.

The possibility that his precious Marylands might be smashed up on the ground grew to be a constant nightmare to the CO of 431 Flight. Shrapnel and air-raid debris lying about on the airfield posed a perpetual threat. Aircraft coming in to land bumped over these jagged bits of metal which quickly mangled tail-wheel tyres to ribbons. Since there were no replacements the maintenance staff was faced with the necessity of making new wheel hubs to fit whatever tyres happened to be in store.

But the mechanics worked marvels of ingenuity with the little they had. They combed over the wrecks of Italian aircraft which had been shot down around Luca, wrenched off the bent and twisted propeller blades and cast new wheel hubs from the salvaged metal. On one occasion during an air raid Whiteley came across three of his men busily filing away oblivious to the lethal uproar going on over their heads. They were manufacturing rivets to fill a much-needed want!

Since they lacked armour plate and fuel tank protection, the Marylands relied on speed, evasion and cloud cover to keep out of trouble. Nevertheless trouble could not always be avoided, particularly during the cloudless days of the late Mediterranean summer.

On the way back from Naples, Italian fighters were always liable to be encountered over Messina, and there were some exciting races with enemy fighter patrols who tried to jump the returning Marylands when the pilots came in over Cape Passero, the southern tip of Sicily, for the customary 'fix'.

The worst problem, however, was getting back into Malta itself. Enemy patrols covered the approaches to the island with the object of intercepting reconnaissance aircraft. If a raid was in progress over Malta, Whiteley and his men relied, for warning of the presence of the enemy, upon Squadron Leader Messenger, the island's devoted Air Controller. As long as their fuel lasted they could hang about over the sea out of harm's way.

Despite Whiteley's repeated injunctions to his aircrews to avoid trouble, their combative instincts could not be entirely suppressed. While returning from a mission Flying Officer Adrian Warburton, one of Whiteley's best pilots, took on an Italian Cant 506 flying boat and shot down his unwieldy opponent. When he gleefully showed Whiteley the photographs he had taken of the enemy plane burning on the water he was a trifle hurt to find himself on the receiving end of a verbal rocket from his CO.

On their next trip this same crew was jumped by enemy fighters off Sicily, but managed to get back to Luca safely. When he climbed aboard to welcome them Whiteley found Warburton, pale and faint, sagging in his seat. Hastily he tore open the pilot's flying jacket and discovered that Warburton had a bullet lodged in his chest.

Fortunately the wound was little more than skin deep, and the pilot soon recovered. The bullet had entered the nose of the Maryland, just missing the navigator's head, and smashed through the instrument panel to find a final resting place in the pilot's body. Luckily by then its force was almost spent.

It was not long after the unit had arrived in Malta that Whiteley noted the navy's special interest in Taranto. By the middle of September he and his aircrews had photographed the base several times.

They were all at once impressed with its possibilities as a target, and from his lowly level Whiteley urged Air Commodore Maynard, the AOC Malta, to arrange for an attack on Taranto by a mixed force of some fifty Beauforts and Blenheim bombers from the United Kingdom. But as the Battle of Britain was then still wavering in the balance, and the highest priority was being given to anti-invasion strikes by Bomber Command, it was scarcely surprising that the suggestion met with a lukewarm response.

When in due course 431 Flight was informed that the navy was planning to attack Taranto with what amounted to little more than a handful of Swordfish the aircrews were aghast. 'The RAF saw it first,' they protested. 'This is one of the finest targets of the war. A small-scale attack will merely scare the Ities and they'll shift their big ships elsewhere.'

But they underestimated the Fleet Air Arm.

At first however Whiteley knew only that the British naval Commander-in-Chief in the Mediterranean particularly desired that a regular watch should be kept upon Taranto. This seemed only natural, since no movements of shipping in the Mediterranean could be planned without the navy knowing what the enemy was doing, where his major naval units were based, and when they left harbour and put to sea.

Then, early in October, the Flight was ordered to step up the frequency of its reconnaissances over Taranto. Thereafter scarcely a day passed without either Whiteley himself or one of his crews looking in on Mussolini's principal naval base.

Not all the hazards of these flights were attributable to the enemy. The weather, too, could be difficult. There was a day for instance when a blanket of fog came down to veil Malta with an opacity reminiscent of London in November. It was a vile day, and the forecast held out little promise of improvement over Taranto. It would probably be cloud all the way.

The duty pilot for this particular sortie was the irrepressible Warburton. As the Maryland took off from Luca and was swallowed up in the humid overhang. 'Warby' cheerfully sang out a warning to his crew. 'Stand by to step out, lads, we're flying at zero feet all the way.' To the navigator he added, 'And you'd better be ready to plot the positions of the ships on a chart if we can't get any pictures.'

The Met report turned out to be only too accurate. There was ten-tenths cloud all the way. Although they flew at a height less than that of a destroyer's bridge they seldom caught a glimpse of the sea. But these conditions merely acted as a challenge to the twenty-two-year old Warburton, as did the state of the battle-scarred aircraft he was flying. Fuselage and wings were sieved through with bullet holes from an encounter with an Italian fighter, and gashed by splinters from a bomb which had exploded nearby while the plane was standing on the airfield at Luca. As they skimmed across the leaden sea the wind whistled dismally through the holes.

The weather was so bad that the Italians did not expect a visit that day. Thus the 'Sardine Tin', as the crew christened the aircraft, was able to fly twice round Taranto's outer harbour before the defences came to life. Then the Italians threw everything they had at the impudent intruder. But by coming down to a low altitude Warburton managed to dodge the flak and, thumbing his nose at the enemy, skimmed off home with a fine selection of pictures in the can.

Mostly however the weather remained clear and conditions were perfect for photography from high altitude. As the days went by many valuable pictures of Taranto were brought back to Malta by 431 Flight. In nearly all of them the major units of the Italian fleet could be seen lying snugly at anchor within the harbour defences.

But more was required of the photographs than a mere cursory scrutiny before being filed away. If they were to yield up all their secrets they needed careful examination by a skilled eye. And for this they had to be despatched elsewhere.

At that early stage in the war photographic interpretation was still in its infancy. Shortly before the aircraft-carrier *Illustrious* arrived in the Mediterranean, RAF Middle East Command had set up its first Interpretation Unit in Cairo. It was to this head quarters, therefore, that the reconnaissance photographs taken by 431 Flight were sent for study by the RAF's budding experts.

Here, too, came one day from the *Illustrious*, a tall dark-haired RNVR lieutenant named David Pollock to learn what he could about this new and promising adjunct to the science of military intelligence.

Pollock was no mere casual student seeking some amusing way of passing the time while his ship lay in harbour at Alexandria. Despite his junior rank and lack of naval experience he was not only the Assistant Staff Officer (Operations) to Admiral Lyster, he was also the carrier's Intelligence Officer. It is probable that he owed both these appointments to his impressive civilian background.

Aged thirty-three at the outbreak of war, Pollock, a solicitor and graduate of Trinity College, Cambridge, was then partner in a law firm who were solicitors to the Bank of England. He was also an enthusiastic yachtsman, a member of the Royal Yacht Squadron, and of the Council of the Yacht Racing Association. In 1936 he had raced for England against Canada in the International 14-foot Dinghy Class. With a love of the sea in his blood it was not surprising that he should join the Royal Naval Volunteer (Supplementary) Reserve, a special section of the RNVR which listed for naval service in the event of war amateur yachtsmen who were prepared to volunteer in peacetime.

But when he received his call-up papers in September, 1939, the Treasury stepped in and claimed his services in connection with the wartime intricacies of exchange control. Having first extracted a promise from the Admiralty that on release from these duties he would be taken into the navy, he was retained to serve on the Economic Policy Committee until after Dunkirk. Then, having managed at last to talk someone else into taking the job, he hastened off to H.M.S. *King Alfred* at Hove to commence his naval service. In due course, sporting the wavy gold stripe of a Temporary Sub-Lieutenant, RNVR, he was appointed to H.M.S. *Illustrious* in August, 1940.

At first Pollock was a trifle scared of his new duties and his impressive sounding title of 'SOO2' on the staff of the carrier's admiral, and was inclined to be blushingly conscious of his Reserve status and inexperience. But he need not have worried. The *Illustrious* was a happy ship and everyone was friendly and helpful.

In particular he found the admiral anything but the unapproachable ogre of his imaginings. When he first entered the great man's cabin in the course of his official business he apologised profusely for disturbing the admiral. To his astonishment he received the warm and somewhat wistful reply, 'My dear Pollock, you are always welcome. You must remember that in any ship the admiral is the most lonely man on board.'

Almost as soon as he joined the carrier, which was then preparing to sail for the Mediterranean, Pollock heard rumours that a big attack was in the wind. Confirmation came shortly afterwards from Admiral Lyster himself, who sent for Thompson and his new assistant and told them, 'The great idea is to attack Taranto.' He instructed them to consult with the commanding officers of the two Swordfish squadrons and draw up a tentative plan for an air assault on the Italian base. This would then be laid before the Commander-in-Chief, Mediterranean, and after his approval had been obtained the aircrews would be given an intensive course of training to fit them for the operation.

But when the *Illustrious* reached the Mediterranean there was other, more immediate, work awaiting the air squadrons.

Pollock had been advised by his naval acquaintances that the quickest way to get on in the Service was to hunt round for some out-of-the-way subject which might conceivably be of use afloat in wartime and specialise in it. Photographic interpretation, about which little or nothing was known in the fleet, seemed to offer plenty of scope, and Pollock decided to interest himself in its possibilities. When the *Illustrious* arrived at Alexandria he learned that the RAF had recently set up a Photographic Interpretation Unit in Cairo. Accordingly he sought and obtained permission from Lyster to attend at the Unit for a short course of study.

There he quickly made friends with the RAF's expert, Flight Lieutenant Idris Jones. But the Unit was as yet meagrely equipped. A whole library of photographs was accumulating and available for study, but there were no instruments or other apparatus to spare for instructional purposes. At Jones's suggestion, therefore, Pollock went out and bought himself a stereoscope, the most useful instrument he would be likely to require. For with a stereoscope two photographs taken from slightly different viewpoints placed side by side can be examined simultaneously to give a three-dimensional effect. Thus minute but possibly vitally important details which might otherwise be overlooked become more readily apparent.

At the conclusion of his five-day course of instruction Pollock returned to his ship, having mastered the first principles of this fascinating new science. His newly acquired knowledge was soon to lead to a discovery of considerable importance to the Taranto plan.

Despite his acceptance as one of themselves by the rest of the ship's officers Pollock still had the feeling that his Reserve status somehow set him apart, and he worked hard to overcome this handicap. He decided that if he could prove that he was fully prepared to face the same dangers as the aircrews his status among them would be enhanced, to their mutual advantage.

One day he bearded Admiral Lyster in his cabin and asked if he might go in the back seat of a Swordfish on a forthcoming raid which was to be made on the enemy's Dodecanese base of Leros. The admiral at once agreed subject to the captain's permission, and Boyd duly gave the project his blessing.

Pollock spent a sleepless and anxious night before the raid, but once the striking force had taken off his fears vanished. During the flight to Leros the air gunner with whom he shared the after cockpit of one of the Stringbags nonchalantly tuned in the wireless set to dance music from an enemy radio station. As Pollock found himself listening appreciatively on another pair of head phones he was astonished at his own sang-froid.

During the actual attack he became so engrossed in what was happening all around him that he forgot to be scared. The multi-coloured enemy flak rising with such deceptive slowness to meet the attackers fascinated him. Some of the tracers appeared to be of a beautiful Cambridge blue. This he thought to be singularly appropriate since he himself had been born and bred in that city and had graduated from her university!

It was only when they landed back on the carrier that Pollock learned how lucky he had been. It had originally been arranged that he should make the flight with 'a nice safe pilot'. But at the last moment Pollock was switched to another Stringbag. The 'nice safe pilot' was shot down and killed in the raid.

Early in October it seemed that Admiral Lyster's impatience to mount the long cherished assault on Taranto was at last to be gratified. The Commander-in-Chief had finally agreed that the attack should take place on the 21st of that month.

But the plan of attack could not be finalised until the latest reconnaissance photographs of Taranto were available. Enquiries made of the RAF in Malta elicited the information that a good set of pictures had been obtained by one of the Marylands of 431 Flight on October 9th, which showed many of the more important Italian ships in harbour. But the negatives and prints had been despatched in the usual way to Cairo.

The matter had now become urgent. Accordingly as soon as the *Illustrious* returned to Alexandria, Pollock was sent off in a Swordfish to Cairo to examine the photographs and bring back the latest report on them.

By virtue of his former attendance as a student at the Photographic Interpretation Unit, Pollock had no difficulty in gaining admission to RAF Headquarters, and quickly sought out Idris Jones. The flight lieutenant willingly produced the required photographs, and Pollock spent the whole of the morning minutely examining them with the aid of his stereoscope as he had been taught.

By placing the prints together a complete panorama of Taranto lay before him. There at their moorings was the enemy fleet – battleships, cruisers and destroyers. Carefully he plotted the gun emplacements and identified and marked the anti-torpedo nets which were suspended from floats around the larger units. Then he searched round for other points of interest.

Over the harbour itself he noticed some irregular lines of white specks which at first he took to be blemishes on the prints. Under the stereoscope, however, the blemishes appeared to stand away from the surface of the water. Further scrutiny of the shore defences along the eastern side of the harbour revealed more of the same kind of white specks. These mysterious dots also recurred on each of the overlapping series of prints. It was obvious, therefore, that they could not be blemishes. Then, in a flash, the explanation came to him. The dots could only be barrage balloons, similar to those which had become a familiar wartime feature around London and other large cities in Britain.

Excitedly he asked Jones to examine the photographs and give his expert opinion. Although the pictures had been taken from a height of 16,000 feet, and neither he nor Jones had seen photographs of barrage balloons before, the flight lieutenant was equally convinced that his erstwhile pupil had stumbled on the right answer.

Pollock knew all about the plan of attack on Taranto, and he also knew from his study of the various intelligence reports they had received that neither Admiral Cunningham nor his staff who had approved the plan suspected that barrage balloons were being employed at the enemy naval base. They expected torpedo nets to be used as the ultimate protection for the ships in harbour. This, then, was a discovery of vital importance, for the whole scheme of attack would have to be drastically altered.

'Look, Jonesy,' he said, 'can I borrow these pictures? I know my admirals, and they're not likely to be convinced by anything a junior RNVR two-striper tells them unless we can produce actual proof.'

'Well, I'd like to help,' said the flight lieutenant dubiously, 'but I'm not allowed to let any photographs be taken out of this office.'

'But this is important,' urged Pollock. 'You've no idea just how important.'

Jones shook his head. 'Maybe,' he said, 'but I just haven't the authority.'

'Well, can't you get it from someone?' pleaded Pollock.

The RAF man considered the point.

'I can ask Groupie,' he said at last.

Group Captain Paynter, the Chief Intelligence Officer, decided however that only the AOC himself could give the necessary permission.

But the Great Man, ironically enough Air Chief Marshal Sir Arthur Longmore who had himself once served as a naval officer, ruled that since the photographs Pollock wanted were the only copies available they must not be removed from the library. And that was that.

Here was dilemma indeed. To Pollock it was imperative that he should take back proof of this startling discovery to his superiors. He stared round the library in exasperation. The filing arrangements were extremely primitive, and the photographs were simply stacked on shelves in a rough semblance of order. The Taranto prints, twenty of them in a packet, were lying on a shelf within reach. They would hardly be missed for twenty-four hours.

He glanced over at Jones. The flight lieutenant was engrosssed in the examination of some pictures spread out on his desk. On a sudden impulse Pollock reached out for the Taranto prints and slipped them into his brief case. Then he rose and strolled to the door.

'Well, I'd better be getting back to the ship with the great news,' he told Jones. 'I'll look in on you again tomorrow. They'll probably want you to give me a written report on that stuff we've been looking at.'

'OK, old man,' murmured Jones, still absorbed in his task. 'Sorry about the pix.'

Once outside the headquarters building Pollock hastened to the airfield, climbed into the waiting Swordfish, and was back on board the *Illustrious* late that afternoon.

Admiral Lyster, he found, had gone ashore, but Captain Boyd was on board. Pollock hurried in to see him, and breathlessly related the story of his discovery. Then he whipped out the photographs he had purloined, and Boyd peered closely at the sinister dots he indicated on each one.

'Well, it looks as though you're right,' he said at last. 'You'd better go over to the flagship right away and show them to the Commander-in-Chief. I'll make a signal to let them know you're coming.'

Within a very short time a somewhat overawed Pollock was mounting to the quarterdeck of the battleship *Warspite* At the head of the flagship's gangway he was greeted by Commander Power, the Staff Officer (Operations) to the Commander-in-Chief himself.

'Now then,' began Power when the two had gone below to the admiral's office, 'what's all this about?'

Once again Pollock told his story and produced the photographs from his brief case.

'Certainly seems that you're on to something,' commented the SO (O) when he had finished. 'Well, you can't see the Commander-in-Chief, but we'll go along and speak to the Chief of Staff.'

At that time Cunningham's Chief of Staff was Rear-Admiral (now Admiral of the Fleet Sir Algernon) Willis. Power knocked and entered the admiral's cabin, reappearing a moment later to beckon Pollock inside. The lieutenant was considerably taken aback to be confronted by a damply naked and rather cross-looking individual, who grunted irritably, 'And what the hell do you want?' Afterwards Pollock discovered that the admiral had been taking a shower preparatory to going ashore for a game of golf.

Somewhat abashed, he explained the reason for his visit and stressed the urgency of the matter. Draping himself in a towel, Admiral Willis sat down at his desk and examined the photographs long and carefully from every angle. Finally he pronounced that he was not entirely convinced. After all, there had been no verifying reports from outside intelligence that the Italians were using barrage balloons. And, of course, photographic interpretation was still a new, unproved and inexact science.

Nevertheless the Chief of Staff was impressed, and he instructed Pollock to return to Cairo and arrange for official RAF confirmation of the interpretation to be sent to the Commander-in-Chief.

This reaction was no more than Pollock had expected, but first he went back to the *Illustrious* and had the precious photographs copied by the carrier's own photographer. Next day he was flown again to Cairo. In the library of the Interpretation Unit he managed to slip the Taranto prints back on to their shelf unobserved. They had not been missed.

In due course an official report confirming the existence of barrage balloons in position at Taranto was sent to Admiral Cunningham, and the plan of assault duly altered to take the new hazard into account.

CHAPTER VI

THE BRIEFING

The wardroom of HMS *Illustrious* was crowded. Forty-two Swordfish pilots and observers sprawled in chairs, squatted on the edges of tables or lounged against the bulkheads. Other officers filled the rest of the available space in the mess. Among them were Pollock and his chief, Commander Thompson; George Beale, the carrier's own Operations Officer, upon whom devolved the duty of briefing and de-briefing aircrews; Ian Robertson, the Commander (Flying); Duckworth, the torpedo officer; Watts, the Met. expert.

Beale was the man of the hour, for he was about to commence the briefing for Operation Judgment.

Prominent among the Swordfish crews were 'Ginger' Hale, 819's CO, placid-faced as ever; Williamson, commanding 815, shorter, fair-haired, slightly tense of feature; 'Tiffy' Torrens-Spence of 819, a Northern Irishman, tall and darkly handsome, a cousin of the renowned 'Stuffy' Dowding, Chief of RAF Fighter Command; and near him 'Alfie' Sutton, his observer; Lieutenants Kiggell and Janvrin of 815, the former a pilot and the latter his observer; Acting Sub-Lieutenant Jack Bowker, also of 815 Squadron, and the most junior sprog in the outfit.

A tall lanky individual in the neat blue uniform of an American naval officer was an interested spectator. He was Lieutenant-Commander Opie, US Navy, unofficially attached to the *Illustrious* so that the American Navy might learn at first hand how the British were fighting their war at sea.

Congress would probably have screamed blue murder had they known of Opie's whereabouts, but the Navy Department in Washington could see farther than the end of a Congressman's nose, and they kept their own counsel. And so the gangling Yank with the twinkling eyes and the friendly grin had become a familiar figure in the British carrier's wardroom.

'Say, Commander, why is the take-off so long between your aircraft?' he asked 'Streamline' Robertson one day during exercises.

'Well, it's only thirty seconds,' replied Robertson defensively.

'I'm pretty sure in our flat-tops they do it in ten,' stated Opie, in no way boastful.

During a subsequent visit to naval headquarters in Cairo he was able to confirm his claim. Robertson thereupon slashed the take-off interval for his pilots in the *Illustrious* by twenty seconds. He wasn't called 'Streamline' for nothing!

There were pilots and observers present, too, who were strangers on board the *Illustrious*, although they and their squadrons – Nos. 813 and 824 – had frequently worked with 815 and 819 on minelaying operations and bombing attacks against the enemy in North Africa and the Aegean. They were the *Eagle* contingent who had been lucky enough to be chosen from among their squadron mates to take part in the long-awaited attack on Mussolini's naval stronghold.

The *Eagles* had been intensely disappointed at the prospect of missing the show. Proud as they were of their big new sister, there was a strong element of rivalry between the aircrews of the two carriers.

For many weary weeks the older vessel had, as her company phrased it, 'carried the can' in the Mediterranean. When Mussolini entered the war the Italian airmen had made many determined attempts to knock out Cunningham's solitary carrier during the British admiral's convoy operations, and the offensive sweeps he had conducted with the object of luring the enemy battle fleet to sea.

Three Sea Gladiators then comprised the *Eagle*'s total fighter strength. But she carried no trained fighter pilots to fly them, for her normal complement of aircraft did not in fact include fighters at all. The Gladiators had been scrounged from a storage depot in Malta by Charles Keighley-Peach, her Commander (Flying).

The *Eagle*'s main air striking power lay in her seventeen Swordfish, which were required to perform the varied functions of torpedo planes, bombers and reconnaissance aircraft. But a faster machine than the lumbering Stringbag was soon found necessary to deal with the Italian reconnaissance planes which maintained a constant watch on the movements of the Mediterranean Fleet.

Flying whichever of the Gladiators happened to be serviceable, Keighley-Peach, himself a former fighter pilot, gallantly tried to protect the fleet single-handed. Whenever an enemy shadower appeared he took off to try to shoot it down or chase it away before the intruder could whistle up his bombers.

On one occasion after a particularly close tangle with the Italians, Keighley-Peach landed on the *Eagle* with his plane badly damaged and a bullet in his thigh. Pausing only to have this wound roughly dressed, he took off again in a refuelled and re-armed Gladiator and eventually shot down one of his opponents.

At every opportunity Keighley-Peach took up volunteers from the Swordfish squadrons to teach them to fly the Gladiators, and instructed them in the rudiments of fighter tactics. Eventually he managed to train two of the Stringbag pilots to his satisfaction, and thereafter the trio accounted for eleven enemy machines between them.

With only seventeen aircraft, less than two squadrons – sometimes, due to the necessity for repair and overhaul of the hard-worked machines, not even one complete squadron – the Swordfish crews of the old carrier performed miracles.

On July 9th, 1940, during the brief clash with the enemy battle fleet contrived by Admiral Cunningham and already related, the *Eagle*'s torpedo-bombers took off in a succession of sub-flights in an attempt to cripple their wary foes and bring them to action, while the carrier herself dodged and swerved under the lash of nine separate high-level bombing attacks. As the fleet was steaming back to Alexandria from this abortive sortie four hundred heavy bombs were hurled at them by the Italian airmen. Fortuntely most of them fell wide.

When, ten days later, the Australian cruiser *Sydney* and five destroyers encountered two Italian cruisers off the coast of Crete and the *Sydney* sank one of them, the second enemy vessel fled. As soon as he heard of this engagement Admiral Cunningham sallied forth from Alexandria in case a larger enemy force should have ventured out in support.

Anticipating that the damaged enemy cruiser which had made her getaway would seek shelter in Tobruk, six of the *Eagle*'s torpedo-bombers were despatched to attack that port. But the cruiser was not in the harbour. The disappointed Swordfish pilots torpedoed an enemy tanker and a number of smaller vessels for good measure.

Then when the Italian army under Marshal Graziani began its build-up in Libya in readiness to invade Egypt, there were fresh targets for the guns of the British fleet and for the Swordfish from the *Eagle*.

In August, while the *Illustrious* was still in the United Kingdom, a sub-flight of three of the *Eagle*'s Swordfish was disembarked to Dekheila while the damaged carrier was herself being patched up in the dockyard at Alexandria. The Stringbags were sent at the request of the Air Officer Commanding, Western Desert, who needed torpedo-bombers to attack enemy ships bringing supplies to Libya.

On the evening of August 21st a patrolling RAF Blenheim reported that an Italian submarine depot ship with a submarine moored nearby, was anchored in Bomba Bay, some miles to the west of Tobruk. Reconnaissance next morning confirmed that the enemy vessels were still at Bomba. Armed with torpedoes, the three Swordfish set out from Sidi Barrani to attack these juicy targets.

Commanding the sub-flight was Captain Oliver ('Ollie') Patch, Royal Marines, Short, slim and wiry, Patch was the only marine in the *Eagle*'s squadrons. He had taken up flying five years after joining the Corps in 1932, and at one time during the dual control period of the Fleet Air Arm by the Admiralty and the Air Ministry he must have set the pundits of nomenclature a problem. For he was a marine holding a RAF commission as a Flying Officer serving in the navy's air arm!

His observer for the flight to Bomba was a young RNVR midshipman named Woodley. The other members of the sub-flight were Lieutenant John Wellham, RN, with Petty Officer Marsh as his observer; and Lieutenant Norman Cheesman, RN, with Sub-Lieutenant (now Captain) 'Satchmo' Stovin-Bradford, RN, as his observer.

As the three Swordfish entered Bomba Bay, flying in line abreast at a height of only thirty feet, they spotted ahead of them an Italian submarine lying on the surface. The U-boat appeared to be charging her batteries, and the crew had obviously taken advantage of their spell in harbour to catch up on their laundry, for a festoon of drying clothes adorned the submarine's jumping wire above the fore and after casing. Farther inshore lay the depot ship, with a destroyer and another vessel alongside.

As soon as they saw the three British planes the Italian sailors who had been lounging about the deck of the submarine raced to their machine guns and opened fire. 'Ollie' Patch weaved violently to fox the gunners. Then, pointing his Swordfish directly at the U-boat, he launched his torpedo from a range of three hundred yards, turned in a tight loop and headed out to sea. The torpedo struck the U-boat squarely beneath the conning tower and sent her to the bottom.

Continuing on towards the three remaining enemy vessels,

Cheesman torpedoed the outermost craft amidships, which blew up and set fire to the destroyer. Wellham ran in on the other side and scored a bullseye on the depot ship, which at once burst into flames.

Except for slight damage to one of the struts of Wellham's aircraft caused by a machine-gun bullet, all the Swordfish made their getaway unscathed. Subsequent reconnaissance photographs showed that all four enemy vessels had been sunk.

After the war 'Ollie' Patch was to meet two of the survivors from the submarine he had sunk in Bomba Bay in August 1940.

'It was lucky for you that you destroyed our ship,' they told him. 'Otherwise we would probably have sunk all your battleships.'

The submarine, he then learned, was the *Iride* which carried a crew of frogmen specially trained in underwater sabotage.

They belonged to the famous Italian Tenth Light Flotilla, whose swimming saboteurs later caused damage to two British battleships in Alexandria harbour and, operating unknown to the Spaniards from a merchantman moored at Algeciras, attacked British merchant ships anchored in Gibraltar harbour.

It was not until after Italy had surrendered that we learned the true extent of the victorious Swordfish attack on Bomba. The submarine *Iride* had been waiting to embark four human torpedoes and their crews for an operation against Alexandria on August 25th. One of the targets scheduled for attack was the *Eagle* herself!

Of these Bomba heroes only two were present in the wardroom of the *Illustrious* on the night of November 11th, Patch and Wellham. With them were nine other *Eagle* aircrew, all experienced in night flying. Lieutenant David Goodwin, Patch's usual observer, was one of these. Except for the brief period during which Patch had been operating from Dekheila he and Goodwin had flown together for over two years, and 'Ollie' no longer commented on his observer's eccentric habit of taking a chamberpot with him on ops!

Two of the *Eagles* were Sub-Lieutenants, William Bull and Stuart Paine. Bull's pilot was Lieutenant Michael Maund, whose grandfather, a railway engineer in Africa, had been a friend of Lobenguela, the famous Matabele chief in the days of Cecil Rhodes. So close had the ties of friendship become between the British engineer and the African chieftain that the elder Maund had christened his son Loben after him. Now the younger Maund, his grandson, had become the worthy exponent of a mode of warfare of which no African warrior could ever have dreamed.

Another member of the *Eagle* group was Lieutenant Gerald Bayly, 'Gerry' to his friends; and with him his navigator and observer, Lieutenant Henry – inevitably 'Tod' – Slaughter, both of 813 Squadron.

Bayly's outward imperturbability gave no indication of the inward qualms he was experiencing. Like the rest of his squadron mates he had undergone a surfeit of operations in the past few weeks, but to him that seemed no reason for the unaccustomed nervousness that beset him. Worse still, he had a premonition about this raid. So jumpy had he felt on the previous night that he had been along to see the doc for some tranquillisers.

But there were others, too, who knew the queasy feeling of 'butterflies in the stomach.'

The briefing in the wardroom of the *Illustrious* on the evening of November 11th was more like an informal after-dinner gathering than the prelude to a battle. In fact, it was scarcely a briefing at all in the accepted sense of the term as we know it today. All the Swordfish crews, including those still on board the *Eagle*, and certainly the entire ship's company of the *Illustrious*, had known for some time that an air attack was to be made upon the Italian battlefleet in their defended harbour of Taranto.

In fact, they had been through almost all of it before when October 21st was originally selected as D-Day for the attack, not only because that date was the anniversary of Trafalgar but because the moon would then be nearing its zenith – an important requirement for the attack. Once this date had been agreed to by the Commander-in-Chief, night exercises for the Swordfish squadrons had been intensified.

Since the carriers had to reach their flying-off positions without detection by the enemy, a long flight to and from the target area was unavoidable for the Stringbags. And this is where the experience of 815 Squadron, who had flown with long-range tanks on their minelaying sorties with Coastal Command proved its value. Fortunately also the *Illustrious* had brought a supply of the tanks out from England with her.

Of sixty-gallon capacity, these were cylindrical metal containers. The only way to carry one in a Swordfish without interfering with the torpedo-release gear however was to strap it into the observer's seat. But this bulky obstruction left no room for the air gunner who was normally carried in a Swordfish. Aircrew for the raid would therefore have to be restricted to pilot and observer only.

Even so, the observer would be very cramped for space, and in addition to suffering this discomfort he was liable to be dowsed with petrol from the tank's overflow pipe when the aircraft took off.

It was while one of these tanks was being fitted that, as previously mentioned, near disaster had come upon the *Illustrious* in the shape of the hangar fire. The aftermath of this mishap was still to be felt.

With the battered *Eagle* out of action and unable to take part in the long-planned Operation Judgment, the *Illustrious* embarked the additional aircraft and crews from her immobilised sister before leaving Alexandria. When she sailed, the bulk of the Mediterranean Fleet went along with her to take up their positions for the complicated series of convoy, transport and warships movements Admiral Cunningham had planned and codenamed 'MB8'.

The first of the four merchant ship convoys, the main body of which was destined for Malta, had sailed from Alexandria on November 5th; and that section of it which was earmarked for Suda Bay was detached in due course.

Three days later Admiral Cunningham, with the battleships *Warspite*, *Valiant*, *Malaya* and *Ramilles*, the *Illustrious* and escorting destroyers, sighted the Malta-bound merchantmen at the rendezvous position, and steamed northwards so as to interpose his force between the convoy and any threat of an Italian attack. In the event no enemy warships did appear, but some Italian bombers came out to attack the British battleships. Fulmars from the *Illustrious* drove them off with the loss of two of their number.

Next day cruisers and destroyers of the British screening force swept the waters around Sicily in search of enemy surface vessels, but the weather was rough and squally and only shadowing enemy aircraft ventured forth to keep an eye on the British ships. Shortly after noon that day a Swordfish took off from the *Illustrious* to carry out routine anti-submarine patrol. And now came an unexpected by-blow from the hangar fire, although no one suspected at the time that this was the cause of the trouble.

Soon after leaving the carrier the Stringbag's engine failed and she force-landed in the sea. The crew was rescued by one of the escorting destroyers.

Early next morning when the fleet was nearing Malta more

Swordfish were sent up on patrol. Not long after they had left the carrier's flight deck a second machine crashed in the sea. Again the crew were rescued, but the aircraft, like that of the day before, was lost.

Then, on the morning of the 11th, a Swordfish of 819 Squadron took off for the routine dawn anti-submarine sweep. The pilot was Sub-Lieutenant Alistair Keith, and his navigator and observer was Lieutenant George ('Grubby') Going. Steadily the Stringbag climbed to fifteen hundred feet, then without warning the engine faltered and died. The *Illustrious* was now twenty miles away.

'What the hell do I do now?' yelled Keith, who had never ditched before, to his observer.

Going, who had, yelled back, 'Glide towards some ships.'

He just had time to tap out an SOS on his radio when the Swordfish pancaked hard. Going was flung head first into the water. But since he struck no obstruction on the way he afterwards referred to his abrupt arrival in the ocean in the extraordinary understatement that it was 'a very comfortable way of ditching.'

As he surfaced he saw that Keith had freed himself and was dragging the dinghy from the sinking plane. The dinghy was duly inflated and the two climbed aboard. Then Going noticed their flame floats bobbing about in the water nearby. He plunged in, scooped up some of them and clambered back into the dinghy. But he had only ignited one float when a boat from the escorting cruiser *Gloucester* arrived to pick them up.

While Keith and Going changed into dry clothing and afterwards sat down to enjoy a second breakfast on board their rescue ship, Robertson in the *Illustrious* was busy probing the cause of the mysterious crashes.

The mishaps, it was discovered, had all occurred to aircraft belonging to 819 Squadron. It was possible that the squadron had been fuelled with contaminated petrol ashore in Alexandria before re-embarking in the carrier. But this was not very probable since the planes had experienced no trouble in flying back on board from Dekheila. Nevertheless assurance must be made.

The tanks of 819's Stringbags were drained and examined. Inside them the investigators found water, sand, and what Robertson described as 'a most peculiar growth looking rather like spaghetti hanging round the baffles, etc.'

Suspicion now pointed to one of the petrol supply tanks on board as being the source of the trouble, especially when Robertson ascertained that 819 Squadron had all refuelled from one particular supply point in the hangar. And, indeed, there were a number of ways in which this tank might have become fouled up.

One of the ships motorboats might have taken in fuel from a contaminated source ashore and passed this back into the carrier's tanks when the boat was drained after being hoisted; or the water and sand had found their way into the tank during the firefighting.

Robertson inclined to the motorboat theory; Boyd to the firefighting. But the matter was never satisfactorily cleared up, for the customary inquiry held on board was overtaken by more important events before a verdict could be arrived at.

Robertson was only too thankful that the trouble had been tracked down in time. Nevertheless three of his precious Swordfish had had to be written off as the price to be paid, and this now reduced the Taranto striking force to twenty-one aircraft.

As the fleet steamed onwards 'Grubby' Going suddenly realised with horror that unless he could somehow get back to the *Illustrious* he would miss the raid. Keith was not earmarked for the attack, but he was just as keen as his observer to rejoin the carrier.

Since Going was the senior of the two flyers he made his way up to the cruiser's bridge and asked the captain if he and his pilot could be sent back to the *Illustrious*. Like other ships of her class the *Gloucester* carried on her athwartships catapult a Walrus amphibian aircraft for use in reconnaissance and gunnery spotting. This could be used as a ferry.

A dedicated flyer and impetuous almost to the point of tactlessness, Going stressed how important it was that he should take part in the raid for which he had been trained, and added unblushingly that anyhow there were relatively few men capable of attacking the Italian fleet!

Captain Rowley regarded the importunate observer with a sardonic eye. But presently he thawed slightly.

'I'll see what I can do,' he promised.

In due course a visual signal was flashed from the *Gloucester* to the *Illustrious*.

'Aircrew think they have an important engagement this evening,' ran the message. 'Am sending them over by Walrus.'

When Going reported his return to Captain Boyd on the carrier's bridge he added a fervent plea that he might still be allowed to go to Taranto.

'Very well,' conceded Boyd after a moment's reflection, 'you may go if you can manage to replace your lost equipment.'

Going was satisfied, for he knew that the gear could easily be replaced. The promise he had wrung from Captain Boyd was in fact a trump card to be held up his sleeve, only to be produced if Doc Keevil should consider grounding him as a result of the morning's ditching. He would also produce it if either Robertson or Beale should try to fob him off with the excuse that all arrangements for the raid had been finalised in his absence and the crews fully made up.

But neither of these eventualities came to pass, and now he, too, stood in the wardroom listening to the briefing alongside his pilot for the raid, Lieutenant Edward Clifford.

However, Going's troubles were not over yet.

Mounting a chair so that he could be seen, Commander Beale recapitulated for his somewhat less than attentive audience the broad outlines of the plan of attack, and emphasised the hazards awaiting them.

These were, in brief, something like 240 ack-ack guns of all calibres which stretegically ringed Taranto; anti-torpedo nets curtaining the Italian battleships; but since these were known to extend down the ships' sides only as far as their maximum draught the torpedoes would be set to run beneath them. Lastly, of course, there were the barrage balloons.

Although Pollock, the SOO2, had discovered the existence of these prior to the original date fixed for the attack in October, the unwelcome news had not in fact been generally made known until that morning. For it was then that a Swordfish from the *Illustrious* had returned from Malta bringing the latest reconnaissance photographs of Taranto, obtained at the navy's request by the obliging Marylands of 431 Flight.

Taken from a height of only 8,000 feet on a gloriously clear day, the photographs revealed not only the five Italian battleships still lying peacefully at their moorings on the sunlit waters of the harbour; they also showed only too clearly those horrid little blobs which the percipient Pollock had earlier suspected and then proved to be balloons.

When the aircrews were handed copies of these latest pictures they crowded round clutching magnifying glasses and stereoscopes, all bent on identifying the sinister objects as anything but what they were.

'Perhaps, it's just ack-ack fire,' suggested one pilot hopefully.

But the lines of blobs were far too regular for the smoke of shellbursts.

The silence of depressed realisation closed down.

At last, 'The bastards!' ejaculated someone in heartfelt tones, and that inelegant epithet accurately summed up the feelings of all present.

Now Beale reminded the assembly of this additional hazard.

But by this time the edge of the threat had become blunted. Muttered Maund of 813 Squadron, 'I don't suppose we shall even see them.'

Others thought likewise, or, more simply, murmured, 'What the hell!'

'The next thing,' went on Beale, having exhausted his catalogue of the trials and tribulations of the fly-in to the target, 'is the return journey.'

But some anonymous philosopher standing at the back drily observed, 'Don't let's bother about that!' And the briefing dissolved into mirth.

As the brass bulkhead clock in the wardroom ticked out the inexorable minutes a mood of quiet elation began to oust the aircrew's customary pre-operation nerves. For, earlier that evening, an almost incredulous piece of news had been wirelessed from Malta to the *Illustrious*.

A Sunderland of the RAF patrolling in the vicinity of Taranto ready to flash a warning message if the prey should suddenly decide to vacate the lair, reported instead that a sixth battleship had entered the harbour.

Now all Mussolini's eggs were in one basket. Why, we can smash the lot, they thought jubilantly.

Comparatively few details remained for Beale to add to what the crews already knew of the forthcoming operation. On the previous afternoon pilots and observers had crowded into the Air Intelligence Office for an explanation of the general plan of attack.

The twenty-one aircraft would be split into two waves, the first comprising twelve and the second nine machines. Robertson had tossed a coin to decide which squadron would go first, and Williamson, CO of 815, had won – or lost, whichever way you chose to regard it. Three of the *Eagle*'s Stringbags would be added to his own nine available aircraft to make up the required twelve. The crews of these would be Maund and Bull, Patch and Goodwin, and Murray and Paine. Kenneth Grieve of 813 would go as observer to Lieutenant Charles Lamb of 815.

Hale of 819 would lead the second wave, due to take off one hour after the first. Bayley and Slaughter, and Wellham and Humphreys of the *Eagle* party would make up numbers for this wave.

Six planes in the first striking force and five in the second would be armed with torpedoes. Four others in the first wave would carry bombs and attack the cruisers and destroyers moored in the inner harbour as a diversion. The remaining two would first drop flares east of the outer harbour, known as the Mar Grande, so as to silhouette the battleships, and then go on to bomb the oil storage tanks for good measure. Of the rest of Hale's wave, two of the Stringbags would dive-bomb the inner harbour, which might then be expected to be in a state of confusion as a result of 815's attentions; the other two would light up the scene with flares once more, and afterwards add their quota of bombs to the oil storage tanks.

Once the composition of the two striking forces had been settled and the order in which they would take off decided, Williamson and Hale retired with their men to work out the specific form of attack each squadron would adopt. Only the outline plan had been given them. How this was to be accomplished was a matter for the respective squadron commanders.

After carefully studying the photographs and the plan of Taranto harbour. Williamson sketched out his strategy. His squadron would approach the enemy stronghold at a height of between eight and ten thousand feet. The leading sub-flight, which would consist of himself and two others, would glide down and attack over the crescent-shaped mole known as the Diga di Tarantola which thrust out into the anchorage from the south-eastern shore of the outer harbour.

The other sub-flight would come in over the harbour from the north-west. Thus they would sandwich the targets between them. If pilots ran into an unexpected volume of ack-ack fire, or a heavy concentration of balloons, they were free to take appropriate action. Each torpedo plane would make its own getaway and return to the carrier independently.

Hale, on the other hand, decided that his best line of approach would be in line astern from the north-west. This would give the Stringbags a straight run in and a nicely spread target, since the enemy battleships appeared to lie in over-lapping berths from this angle. Thus if a torpedo veered slightly off course it would be almost certain to hit something worthwhile in the crowded anchorage.

There were just two drawbacks to this plan.

The glide-in would bring the torpedo-droppers uncomfortably close to the concentration of anti-aircraft guns sited on either side of the canal which connects the outer and inner harbours. Also they would have to go down over the top of a line of balloons which were moored on barges to the west of the anchored ships.

But these risks, Hale decided, were acceptable, and his men agreed. In fact, they thought Williamson's scheme the more hazardous of the two.

As they listened now to Beale the two squadron commanders mentally ran over their plans once more. Quiet and unassuming himself, Williamson would be leading a dashing crowd, for that was the reputation 815 Squadron had acquired under Kilroy, their former CO. He was a trifle worried about those balloons. However, from the photographs he judged them to be spaced about three hundred yards apart, while the wingspan of a Swordfish was a little less than sixteen yards. The odds were therefore in favour of being able to pass through without hitting anything.

Duckworth, too, had worked out on his slide rule the mathematical chances of hitting a cable. They were, he declared, ten to one against.

'Ginger' Hale felt completely calm. The thought of those balloons still bothered him a little, too, but he had decided to take his Swordfish right down on the deck when they arrived. Then he could dodge round the barges and thus avoid the cables that carried the damn gasbags.

But at the back of his mind lurked the unpleasant thought that the ship's company of the carrier was firmly convinced that none of the Swordfish would return from the raid. Well, he had buttoned up that eventuality, too. For there was a special letter he had written to his wife sealed and addressed in his cabin He hoped she wouldn't have to read it though.

In the meantime the hangar of the carrier was a hive of industry. Fitters and riggers swarmed over the squatting Swordfish, the bluish-green paint on the wings and fuselages of the aircraft gleaming dully under the brilliant electrics in the hangar roof.

Two days previously one of the Swordfish of 815 had been damaged through making a heavy landing. Maintenance crews had been working feverishly ever since to restore the Stringbag to serviceability for the raid. Triumphantly they completed their task with just over an hour to spare before take-off.

Petrol tanks were topped up to capacity, and the overload tanks filled up with their extra sixty gallons. Only the torpedo-dropping Swordfish carried this bulky obstruction in the after cockpit. The bombers and flare-droppers had theirs strapped on externally since they had no torpedoes to worry about. Self-sealing fuel tanks for aircraft were then unknown, but the airmen preferred not to think overmuch about the added risk if they should run into enemy night fighters on the way.

Torpedoes, bombs and flares were next brought into the hangar for the final task of arming the Stringbags. The phosphor-bronze warheads of the torpedoes had been filmed over with a thin coat of oil as a preservative, and this greasy surface inevitably lent itself, much as would a steamy window pane, for odd dood-lings by the mechanics.

Upon them, therefore, they inscribed appropriate messages to the eventual recipients as they slung the torpedoes into position between the legs of the aircraft. 'To Musso from Winnie,' proclaimed one gleaming load of death; 'Best Wishes from *Illustrious* and *Eagle*,' said another.

The most important item in the preparation of the 'fish' for their deadly task had been the insertion into their warheads of a new firing device known as the Duplex pistol. The *Illustrious* had brought out with her from England the first batch of these to be issued for service in the Mediterranean.

A British invention developed shortly before the outbreak of war by torpedo specialists in HMS *Vernon*, the pistol was designed to be operated by the magnetic field of any ship be-neath which it passed; the same principle, in fact, as the Germans were using in their magnetic mine. Since the pistol was also capable of exploding on impact it was given the name 'Duplex'.

This new weapon was intended for use both by aircraft and submarines, but a number of faults still remained to be ironed out when the war began. The pistol's chief defect was that it was liable to be affected by the earth's magnetic field when running in a swell and thus cause a premature explosion.

Both airmen and submariners distrusted the pistol for this reason, and its use for the Taranto attack was approved only after considerable opposition had been overcome.

Dropping a torpedo itself with any hope of success was already sufficiently tricky. The aircraft had to be in level flight, or slightly nose down, at an altitude of about 150 feet, pointing directly at the target; and the torpedo had to be dropped in a depth of five fathoms of water or more. The slightest devia-tion of the plane at the moment of release might send the torpedo off course, cause it to dive straight to the bottom, or even to break up altogether.

Duckworth, the Torpedo Officer, was one of those who stressed the advantages of the Duplex pistol. There would be no swell in Taranto harbour, he pointed out, and torpedoes so armed would explode beneath the enemy ships where they were most vulnerable and with added destructive force. He was strongly supported by Boyd, who had known about the weapon from the early days of its development when he himself commanded the *Vernon*.

But the use of the pistol added certain difficulties to the attack. Due to the comparative shallowness of the water in Taranto harbour the torpedoes would have to be set with delicate precision so that they would run at the right depth between the harbour bed and the bottoms of the enemy ships without grounding or firing prematurely.

Also the pistol was so designed that the torpedo would only become dangerous after it had travelled several hundred yards. This was known as the safety range. Because of the short runs the Swordfish pilots would have to make due to the hazards through which they must fly to drop the missiles, there was a danger that the torpedoes might pass beyond their targets. Yet with no safety range at all the 'fish' might explode beneath the dropping aircraft as soon as they struck the water, or soon afterwards, due to oscillation.

But the airmen were determined to leave nothing to chance to ensure success in their mission, and they prevailed upon Duckworth to run off several dozen yards of the safety range before the torpedoes were loaded on to the Stringbags.

The aircraft detailed to make the diversionary attacks were armed with six 250-lb. semi-armour piercing bombs each; the flare-droppers with sixteen parachute flares apiece, set to ignite at varying heights. They would also carry four bombs.

While the armourers were securing the bombs and flares in position beneath the aircraft wings, Bill Hayter, the carrier's Torpedo Gunner, appeared in the hangar hefting a pair of marine's steel-shod marching boots. He searched round for Ollie Patch's plane, then solemnly lashed the boots to one of Patche's SAP bombs.

The Marine detachment of the *Illustrious* had decided that the solitary representative of their famous Corps to take part in the raid would be the most appropriate messenger to convey to Mussolini their own special contribution to his fleet's dis-

TARANTO

MAR
PICCOLO

Cruisers

Cape Rondinella

Commercial
Basin

Cruisers & Destroyers

Bombs

TARANTO

Seaplane
Base

Cruisers

MAR
GRANDE

Cavour

Cavour

Littorio

Littorio Cavour

San Pietro
Island

Destroyers

Cavour

San Paolo
Island

Floating
Dock

Oil Storage
Tanks

Guardships

Diga di Tarantola

Breakwater

Cape San Vito

Submerged Breakwater

⚲ Balloon Barrage
× Net Defences
⊛ A.A. Batteries
↓ Torpedo Dropping Positions

Miles

Taranto harbour, showing the Italian battleships at anchor in the
outer harbour behind their defences of anti-torpedo nets and barrage
balloons. Arrows show the aircraft torpedo dropping positions.

comfiture. Patch was afterwards to comment that the boots probably wreaked more damage than his bombs!

At 6 p.m., on the evening of November 11th, the *Illustrious* and her escort, which comprised the cruisers *Gloucester*, *Berwick*, *Glasgow* and *York*, and four destroyers, were detached from the main fleet and, turning north-east, headed towards the Greek island of Cephalonia. They were obeying Cunningham's laconically signalled instruction to Admiral Lyster, 'Proceed in execution of previous orders for Operation Judgment.' As senior officer commanding the Judgment Force, Lyster was at last to launch from his own flagship the long-planned air attack upon the Italian enemy.

While the *Illustrious* and her consorts settled down on their new course, Lyster descended from the carrier's bridge and made his way below to the crowded wardroom.

To some of the younger members of the assembled aircrews the carrier admiral had always appeared to be a somewhat aloof and formidable figure – an impression admirals are apt to make on junior officers. But those who knew him better, men like Hale, Torrens-Spence, Robertson, Sutton, Going and George Beale, all of whom had served with him in the *Glorious*, affectionately dubbed him 'Daddy' Lyster. True he was tough and demanded a high standard of his subordinates, but he never asked the impossible.

His somewhat forbidding demeanour masked in fact a dry and lively sense of humour. After he became Fifth Sea Lord at the Admiralty in April, 1941, he one day inspected a naval air station at which his daughter was serving as a Wren.

There was considerable speculation among the personnel of the station as to what the admiral would do when he beheld his offspring standing among her colleagues in the drawn-up ranks. Would he stop and speak, or would he ignore her?

But when finally he came opposite his daughter he did pause. 'And what is your name?' he asked.

'Lyster, sir,' replied the Wren smartly, standing stiffly to attention, eyes firmly to the front.

'Ah, yes,' nodded the poker-faced admiral. 'I remember. I met your mother about eighteen years ago.'

But now Lyster had something rather less drily humorous to say to the young men who stood facing him in the carrier's wardroom. A pep talk, they called it. But first there was a message from Admiral Cunningham to read to them.

'Good luck, then, to your lads in their enterprise,' the Commander-in-Chief had signalled. 'Their success may well have a most important bearing on the course of the war in the Mediterranean.'

And this, too, was the gist of the few, well-chosen words Lyster spoke to the men whose progress he had watched and in whose future he had so much faith.

'Go to it,' he ended, 'and good luck!'

On his way up to the flight deck after the briefing Lieutenant Charles Lea, of 819 Squadron, encountered Lyster in a narrow gangway. The lieutenant stood to one side to allow his admiral to pass. But Lyster paused.

'Good luck, Lea,' he said. Then with a twinkle he added, 'I want you to kick them in the pants because the admiral in command at Taranto once had the audacity to kiss me on both cheeks, and I didn't like it!'

'Aye, aye, sir,' grinned the airman. 'I'll do my best.'

CHAPTER VII

FLEET IN PORT

On the evening of November 11th, Admiral Domenico Cavagnari sat as usual at his desk in the Ministry of Marine, in Rome.

The admiral was a busy man, for in addition to being Chief of the Italian Naval Staff he was also Under-secretary of State for the Navy. Thus the entire responsibility for running the Ministry as well as Mussolini's fleet rested on his shoulders.

But Cavagnari, a dark-haired, hatchet-faced man with a small black moustache, was a glutton for work, and he possessed the physical stamina to back up his labours. For he was seldom known to take more than five hours' sleep at night, and was at his desk early and late. Regarded as an able, pertinacious individual, Cavagnari enjoyed a high reputation in Italian naval circles.

In a few hours time that reputation was due to be severely jolted.

Inside a separate wing of the Ministry, entry to which was permitted only upon production of a special pass, the rooms and corridors were alive with activity throughout day and night. For here was housed Supermarina, the supreme operational headquarters of the Italian Navy.

In administrative control of this throbbing nerve centre was Cavagnari's deputy, sleek monocled Admiral Odoardo Somigli. Under his orders three junior flag officers headed the main sections whose staffs, working continuously in twenty-four-hour watches, controlled and co-ordinated the activities of the Italian fleet.

By virtue of its functions Supermarina also formed the core of an intricate telephone, telegraph and radio network which linked all naval commands throughout the mainland and in the island of Sicily. Urgent messages could thus be transmitted to these commands by direct and secret lines. Constant touch was maintained by radio with ships at sea and in overseas bases.

Ever since its participation in Marconi's first successful experiments with wireless telegraphy at the beginning of the century, the Italian Navy had spent a great deal of time and money in building up a first-class system of communications.

Thus by 1940 Supermarina was equipped with every modern device in this specialized field. More than three million messages were handled by its staff alone during the war.

By reason of the information which constantly streamed in by day and night the staff officers who manned Supermarina's operations room could pinpoint the precise position of every ship in the Italian Navy at any given moment. They also kept careful track of the movements of enemy naval units.

In its coding and cypher officers Mussolini's secret war moves were revealed to the select few who handled the cypher and code books.

Staffed by a team of experts, Supermarina's cryptographic section had managed to break down and unravel the secrets of British naval reconnaissance signal procedure. Profiting by this new-found ability to read their enemy's coded messages, they were able to offset some of the Italian Navy's deficiencies in aerial reconnaissance.

Supermarina was a competent organisation and it worked well. But it was bogged down with paper work, and its operational control of the fleet was fettered by the directives of the Supreme Command, which was dominated by the army who understood little about the strategical and technical problems of naval warfare. More important, perhaps, its efficiency suffered from the chronic lack of co-operation between the Regia Aeronautica and the Italian Navy.

On the night of November 11th the plot at Supermarina showed that six battleships, nine cruisers, and several *squadrillas* of destroyers and fleet auxiliaries, together with a number of merchant ships, were berthed in the twin harbours of Taranto. In overall command of this large assembly of ships was Admiral Inigo Campioni, the fleet commander, flying his flag in the newly completed 35,000-ton battleship *Vittorio Veneto*.

Campioni's original squadron of three battleships had been reinforced by three more which, together with a number of cruisers and destroyers, had been withdrawn from the Adriatic, Naples and Sicily commands. The eventual destination of this powerful fleet had not been officially decided, but there were rumours that it would shortly be sailing in support of a landing on the Greek island of Corfu.

In the opinion of some of the more farseeing staff officers at Supermarina the congregation of all the principal units of Italy's fleet at Taranto was a risky proceeding. For there was an ever-present possibility that the enemy might attempt a torpedo attack on the port from the air.

That their fears were by no means groundless had already been unpleasantly demonstrated when on July 10th the fleet destroyer *Pancaldo* was torpedoed and sunk in harbour at Augusta by aircraft of the British Fleet Air Arm following Campioni's abortive clash with Cunningham off Calabria.

Although few of the more senior Italian naval officers seriously thought that the British would have the temerity to try to attack a major enemy fleet in its own harbour, certain precautions were put in hand. Chief of these was an order placed by the Ministry of Marine for more protective anti-torpedo nets to be manufactured and supplied to all naval bases. Some 14,000 yards were to be earmarked for use at Taranto alone.

But when Mussolini blithely plunged his country into war he was so convinced that hostilities would be over in a matter of months that Italian industry was still allowed to trail along at peacetime tempo. Thus only about 3,800 yards of the necessary netting was emerging from the factories each month.

Yet even if the netting had been immediately available it is doubtful if Supermarina's orders for its use would have been followed to the letter.

The senior officers of the fleet were far more concerned about ensuring freedom of manoeuvre for their ships. To haul up and re-lay hundreds of yards of heavy, cumbersome steel netting every time their ships proceeded in and out of harbour was far too fatiguing and time-wasting.

More than three thousand yards of anti-torpedo netting were therefore allowed to accumulate rust in the dockyard storehouses at Taranto.

But the overall protection of his ships whilst they were in harbour was not the principal concern of Admiral Campioni. Responsibility for the defences of Italy's premier naval port was a matter for the Port Admiral, or local Commander-in-Chief. This worthy was Admiral Arturo Riccardi, a kindly natured individual of strong religious convictions.

Riccardi secretly entertained a great admiration for the British Navy. When in 1938 he paid an official visit to Malta in command of an Italian naval squadron, he proudly pointed out to British visitors to his flagship a copy of Southey's *Life of Nelson*, which he said he always kept on his bedside table.

Admiral Cunningham, at that time second in command of the Mediterranean Fleet, who was thus one of Riccardi's hosts, and eventually became his wartime opponent, later commented that the Italian admiral's subsequent actions showed that he had not greatly benefited by his nightly reading!

The naval port of Taranto, lying at the head of the Gulf of the same name, well within the arch of the Italian 'boot,' comprises an inner and outer harbour which are known respectively as the Mar Piccolo and the Mar Grande. The two are connecetd by a short narrow channel.

The Mar Piccolo is thus almost landlocked, and the naval dockyard is situated along its southern shore, together with the necessary pens and jetties for berthing cruisers, destroyers and smaller craft.

The Mar Grande is a spacious anchorage, almost twelve square miles, which opens out to the westward and is protected by long, partly submerged breakwaters. These, together with the large island of San Pietro and the smaller San Paolo islet nearby, almost entirely enclose the natural bay formed by Cape Rondinella to the north and Cape San Vito to the south. Taranto itself, a town of some 140,000 inhabitants, lies behind the dockyard which provides the greater part of the population with their livelihood.

The whole of the port area was ringed and honeycombed with anti-aircraft defences capable of concentrating a massive volume of gunfire into the air space above.

Twenty-one batteries of 4-inch high-angle guns were strategically sited to deal with high-flying aircraft. These were backed up by nearly two hundred pom-pom guns and close-range weapons. Twenty-four of these were heavy machine guns in special mountings, and there were over a hundred light automatic weapons sited in positions ashore and afloat.

This impressive array of ordnance could be supplemented if necessary by the guns of those warships which happened to be in harbour. There was a co-ordinated fire plan for ships and shore defences, but normally the latter assumed responsibility for dealing with air raids on the port. Ships only opened fire if individually attacked.

The air raid early warning system consisted of a number of batteries of sensitive sound-locators set up in groups, which were known as 'airphonic stations'. Thirteen of these airphonic stations, linked by direct telephone to the headquarters of Fortress Command, ringed the area and maintained a constant listening watch on all the approaches to Taranto.

In the case of air attack at night nests of searchlights would be brought into action to assist the guns' crews to pinpoint enemy raiders. More than a score of long-range searchlights were sited in and around the twin harbours. Some of these were mounted in installations ashore and others on pontoons moored in the anchorage itself. Additional illumination could also be provided if required by searchlights from the ships in port.

Should any enemy airman nevertheless manage to succeed in penetrating these formidable defences he would encounter a further hazard in the shape of a balloon barrage.

But on the night of November 11th only twenty-seven balloons were in fact in place. Suspended from long steel cables, twenty of them, positioned in V formation, covered the south-eastern approach to the battleship anchorage in the Mar Grande. Ten were spaced along the south-eastern shoreline, and the other ten floated from pontoons moored along the length of the Diga di Tarantola, the curved mole marking the southern limit of the anchorage inside the harbour. The remainder of the balloons, suspended from lighters or barges, covered the seaward approach to the cruiser anchorage in the centre of the Mar Grande.

Normally there would have been many more of these aerial obstacles in position. But the storms and high winds which had recently battered southern Italy had destroyed as many as sixty of Taranto's barrage balloons, and it had been impossible to replace them. The necessary hydrogen for inflating the gas-bags was scarce, and none was available at short notice – another consequence of Mussolini's hasty participation in a war for which the country was not fully prepared.

Despite the shortcomings in the matter of nets and barrage balloons, however, Admiral Riccardi and his brother flag officers were confident that the defences of Taranto were nevertheless sufficiently fearsome to deter the most resolute enemy.

Along with his colleagues in Supermarina, Riccardi was equally well aware that torpedo attack from the air might be attempted against the port which he commanded. But, like them, he expected to receive prior information from the air force in good time of any threatening lunges by the British fleet.

If an enemy aircraft-carrier attempted to approach within striking distance of the Italian mainland she would be spotted and reported by air reconnaissance long before she could reach the required position for launching her aircraft. Bombers and surface naval forces would then make short work of the venture-some intruder.

Yet with the opening of the Greek campaign by Mussolini

the threat of enemy air attack had become greater, since the Greek Government had placed their airfields at the disposal of the RAF. Curiously enough, it was the Italian Army Command who became jittery about the safety of the fleet at Taranto and considered that it should be moved from that port.

But in addition to preparing for the possible foray against Corfu, Admiral Campioni had another and more urgent reason for keeping his ships where they were.

For several days past information had been coming in concerning enemy naval movements in the Mediterranean. Reliable Italian agents in Gibraltar had reported that a British force had sailed eastwards on the evening of November 7th. From other sources came messages informing Supermarina that four battleships and an aircraft-carrier had left Alexandria on the previous day, steering westward.

Campioni made ready on the 7th to sally forth with his fleet to meet any possible British threat, but the further enemy sighting reports he expected to receive failed to materialise.

It was not until the afternoon of that day that Italian reconnaissance aircraft radioed any fresh information about the enemy's movements. But by this time the convoy which they had earlier sighted in the central Mediterranean heading towards Malta was out of reach of the Italian battle fleet.

That same evening reconnaissance planes reported sighting the Alexandria force again. The British ships were now south of the Malta-bound convoy and steaming southwards. But the information given was so meagre that a striking force of twenty-five Italian bombers despatched to attack the retiring British failed even to locate them.

That night, however, Supermarina ordered nine additional submarines to sea, and despatched a number of torpedo boats to patrol off Malta.

Next day the muddle continued. The Gibraltar force was reported to have reversed its course. Conflicting and highly confusing messages came in about the movements of the British warships which had sailed from Alexandria. From an exasperated summary they made of these reports Supermarina in Rome, and Campioni waiting in harbour at Taranto with steam up, could only assume that this particular enemy squadron must now be a long way from Taranto and apparently returning to base.

The inadequacy of Italian air reconnaissance was further demonstrated when on the following morning observation posts in Pantellaria and Linosa reported sighting a group of enemy warships steaming past those islands. It was concluded that these ships must have been detached from the Gibraltar formation and crossed the Sicilian Channel during the night.

Then on November 10th, with typical inattention to the necessary vital details, Italian reconnaissance aircraft reported sighting a group of ships of unknown type and number proceding eastwards from Malta. Next morning these ships were again sighted almost in the same position, but bombers which were sent out to attack them failed to find this tempting target.

This seems to have been all the information received by Supermarina about Cunningham's Operation 'MB8' and passed on by them to Admiral Campioni. Thus the powerful Italian fleet continued to sit passively in port, completely unaware of the lightning that was about to strike it.

The six battleships were moored in the Mar Grande in a rough semi-circle. The four *Cavour*-class, the *Conte di Cavour* herself, *Caio Duilio*, *Cesare* and *Andrea Dorea*, each armed with ten 12.6-inch guns, lay within three-quarters of a mile of the shore. A little farther out the two new 15-inch-gun monsters *Vittorio Veneto* and *Littorio* lay between their head and stern buoys. A number of destroyers shared the same stretch of water.

In the cruiser anchorage towards the centre of the harbour fenced around by a rectangle of anti-torpedo nets – part of which also enclosed the battleship anchorage – lay the three 8-inch-gun cruisers *Cara*, *Fiume* and *Gorizia*.

Inside the Mar Piccolo two more 8-inch-gun cruisers lay at buoys in midstream. They were the *Trieste* and *Bolzano* which had been brought round from Palermo to join Campioni. Four destroyers were moored to buoys nearby. Secured stern-on to the pens and jetties of the naval dockyard were four 6-inch-gun cruisers and seventeen fleet destroyers.

Also berthed in the inner harbour were five torpedo boats, sixteen submarines, four minesweepers and a minelayer, together with supply and hospital ships and tankers. In the commercial basin lay a number of tugs and merchant ships.

As the sun dipped towards the west in the early evening of November 11th, the townspeople of Taranto went about their normal affairs as usual. Workmen streamed out of the dockyard gates at the end of their day's labour and threaded their way along the narrow streets together with homeward-bound factory hands and office workers. Some called in at their favourite *osteria* to drink a glass or two of vino and gossip for a while about the war with soldiers and sailors of the garrison forces and from the ships in port on leave. Strollers along the seafront paused to gaze proudly at the anchored fleet mirrored on the sunlit waters of the Mar Grande.

The battleships and cruisers lay peacefully at their moorings, with their booms out and boats tied up alongside. Naval motorboats sped fussily on routine business between the warships, leaving broad white wakes to fan out on the calm surface of the water.

When darkness had fallen a few hours later the moon rose, shedding a silvery radiance over the quiet scene. Except for an occasional patrolling policeman the streets were empty and deserted, and no lights shone from the shuttered houses. A strict blackout system was in force, and underground air raid shelters had been erected in which the townsfolk could take cover when an air raid alert was sounded. So far, however, Taranto, unlike the Adriatic ports of Brindisi and Otranto, had suffered little from enemy air attack.

Anti-aircraft gun and searchlight crews lounged in their shelters, smoking, yarning and card-playing. Sentries strolled up and down in the moonlight, or huddled in corners in their greatcoats, for once the sun had gone the air struck chill.

There had been many nights like this since Mussolini had thrown in his lot with Hitler, and there was no indication that the night of November 11th would be any different from the others.

No indication, that is, until five minutes to eight p.m.

At that moment a telephone bell shrilled in the room of the duty officer at the headquarters of Fortress Command. A distant airphonic station reported that they had picked up the sound of an unidentified aircraft to the south of their position.

Probably just another enemy reconnaissance mission, thought the duty officer as he acknowledged receipt of the warning. There had been a good many of these in the last few days. But very little happened as a rule. There was no reason to suppose that this was anything but yet another wandering snooper. Nevertheless in accordance with orders he alerted the batteries.

The report he had received stated that the aircraft detected on the sound locators appeared to be approaching the land near the south-eastern arm of the gulf, many miles from Taranto. As no immediate follow-up report came in, the duty officer did not consider it necessary to alarm the civilian population by sounding the general air raid warning. He relaxed and lit a cigarette.

Twelve minutes later more messages began to come in to Command Headquarters. 'Suspicious noises' were reported by a number of airphonic stations in the outer ring of defences. This was more urgent.

The duty officer snapped into action. He contacted the Fortress Commander and ordered the alarm to be sounded in the town. Within a few minutes the stillness of the night was rent by the banshee wail of sirens.

The anti-aircraft gunners swung their weapons round to cover the line of approach expected to be taken by any enemy aircraft which might be making for the port. On board the warships at anchor and alongside in the dockyard gun-crews went to action stations. Ashore the townspeople scurried along to the air raid shelters.

But the night remained quiet. In the moonlight the superstructures of the warships in the Mar Grande cast quivering black shadows on the water, and above the houses in the town the belfry of the old cathedral stood out as prominently as at noonday.

Abruptly the staccato bark of anti-aircraft guns shattered the silence. The Fifth Battery Group at Grottaglie had opened fire. An intruder was approaching, but a few rounds sufficed to scare off the enemy plane. Soon the listening posts reported the sound of aircraft engines rapidly diminishing. A few minutes later the all-clear was sounded.

But the respite was brief.

At nine p.m., further suspicious noises were reported from the Santa Maria di Luca area. This was some seventy miles away, and the Fortress Commander was fairly sure now that the troublesome intruder was merely a single aircraft from Malta patrolling the Gulf. But when one was concerned with the safety of an important port like Taranto it was as well to take no chances. He ordered a second alert to be sounded.

The Fortress Commander's assumption was in fact correct. An RAF Sunderland aircraft of No. 228 Squadron, Middle East Command, was indeed patrolling off Taranto. Piloted by Wing Commander (now Air Marshal Sir Gilbert) Nicholetts, the crew of Sunderland L.5807 had an important mission to perform.

For if any of the Italian capital ships should make a move

to leave Taranto that night it was their job to flash the news to the *Illustrious* at once.

But Campioni's fleet had no intention of sailing, and the only consolation granted to Nicholetts and his crew for their ten-hour vigil was a grandstand view of the events which were to make that night a memorable one.

But none of this was known to the Italians.

For more than an hour no further reports of approaching aircraft were received by Taranto's fortress headquarters. Yet the alert was not cancelled. Anti-aircraft Command began to entertain hopes that nothing further would develop. Relieved by the long silence the townsfolk began to move out of the shelters and creep home to bed.

Yet the Fortress Commander was still apprehensive. He had a feeling that a troublesome night lay ahead. His suspicions were confirmed when at ten twenty-five further warnings began to come in from the outer ring of listening posts.

Three reports of air activity within the space of two hours seemed to presage an enemy raid on the port. He ordered a check to be made on the readiness of the defences.

The Italians did not know it, but the sound of aircraft engines which were now being picked up by their airphonic stations was not coming from the earlier intruder. Nicholetts' patrolling Sunderland.

The first striking force from the *Illustrious* had been in the air for nearly two hours, and was now barely forty-five miles from Taranto.

At ten minutes to eleven the air raid sirens in the town wailed once more. The crews of the anti-aircraft guns in the San Vito area trained their weapons towards the south-east. In the moonlight the gaping gun muzzles looked like clusters of blank staring eyes. Suddenly they flashed flame, and the thunder of barrage fire shook the town.

CHAPTER VIII

THE FIRST STRIKE

FLANKED on either side by her escort of cruisers and destroyers, HMS *Illustrious* knifed through the dark waters of the Ionian Sea at twenty knots. The three-quarter moon hung in the sky almost directly astern of the speeding ships, its shining beams flecking their creamy wake with a myriad points of silver.

On the compass platform of the carrier Boyd was feeling a little worried, for although night flying conditions were perfect there was practically no surface wind. This would make take-off difficult, since the aircraft would all be very heavily laden with long-range fuel tanks, torpedoes and bombs. The ship would probably have to be worked up to full speed to create the thirty-knot wind over the deck necessary to get them off.

Below the island and aft on the carrier's shadowy flight deck the first strike of Swordfish was being ranged, wings folded to enable all twelve to be fitted into the limited space available. They looked, in the words of one of the pilots, 'more like four-poster bedsteads than front-line aeroplanes.'

No wonder Opie had exclaimed when he first beheld a Swordfish, 'My God, you don't mean to say you fly those things!'

Only the letters and figures painted on the fuselage of each machine differentiated one Stringbag from another - except in the eyes of the aircrews, to each of whom his own machine possessed its special points of familiarity.

All aircraft belonging to the *Illustrious* squadrons bore the identifying initial letter L; those of the *Eagle* the letter E.

Williamson, 815s squadron commander, would thus be piloting Swordfish L.4A, with Lieutenant Norman ('Blood') Scarlett as his observer. L.4C would have Sub-Lieutenant Philip Sparke, DSC, at the controls, and Sub-Lieutenant Johnny Neale in the rear seat.

L.4R also carried a brace of sub-Lieutenants as aircrew: August Macauley, RN, piloting, and Tony Wray of the RNVR, behind. L.4K was piloted by Nazi-hating Lieutenant Neil Kemp, with Sub-Lieutenant Ronald Bailey as observer; L.4M by Lieutenant Henry Swayne, with Johnny Buscall, another RNVR Sub., in the after cockpit. L.4P would have Lieutenant Launcelot Kiggell at the stick, with Hugh Janvrin, a massive and laconic six-footer jack-knifed in the observer's seat; and L.5B piloted by Lieutenant Charles Lamb, was taking Grieve of the *Eagle*'s 813 Squadron as observer.

Kiggell and Lamb comprised the 'lighting-up party'. They would first drop the all-important flares, and then endeavour to set Taranto's oil storage tanks ablaze with bombs.

L.4L was piloted by Sub-Lieutenant Bill Sarra, with Jack Bowker in the rear seat; and L.4H by Sub-Lieutenant Tony Forde, with Anthony Mardel-Ferreira, a Sub-Lieutenant RNVR, as observer.

Of the *Eagle* aircraft, Lieutenant Maund, with William Bull, his sub-Lieutenant observer, of 813 Squadron, would be flying E.4F, now fully restored to serviceability after her airscrew and lower main plane had suffered damage when Maund accidentally rammed the carrier's crash barrier during exercises.

Ollie Patch of 824 Squadron would be piloting E.5A, while David Goodwin, complete with chamberpot, occupied the observer's cockpit; and John Murray, a lieutenant, also of 824 in E.5Q, with Sub-Lieutenant Stuart Paine as observer.

While Williamson and his six torpedo-bombers were gliding down on the enemy battle fleet it would be the task of Parch, Forde, Murray and Sarra to divert the attention of the Italian cruisers and destroyers moored in the Mar Piccolo.

II

Before the fully armed Swordfish were transferred from hangar to flight deck the pilots had anxiously inspected their machines, checking the already checked. Torpedoes had been drop-tested by releasing them back on to the loading trolleys; cockpit and navigation lights tested, and emergency rations and water checked over.

This last was something more than merely normal pre-flight routine, for all raid plans of the two Swordfish squadrons included an outline escape scheme for the benefit of any unfortunates who might be shot down. The scheme covered an agreed rendezvous, a hideup, and a possible mode of getaway; and for this food and water were vital.

No one voiced the thought on this particular night that the chances of escape from such a strongly defended area as Taranto might be exceedingly slim.

While the carrier worked up speed and Boyd sniffed vainly for a breath of wind, the aircrews sat at dinner in the wardroom, along with the rest of the ship's officers who were not on duty. Tonight the Swordfish boys were the special favourites of the Maltese chief steward, for were they not about to kick the backside of the insufferable Mussolini?

The crews ate soberly. They had a flight of not less than four hours ahead of them, with the return trip probably taking even longer than the outward journey.

Bayly of 813 found it particularly difficult to force down the food he knew he must east. Cursed with an imagination more vivid than most, he was unable to wrench his mind away from the terrors that might lie ahead. Tonight his pre-operational nerve flutter seemed worse than usual.

All the Swordfish crews drank more coffee than was customary. Afterwards they smoked cigarettes with jerky, nervous gestures, and wandered about the wardroom anteroom sipping at their cups and chatting aimlessly.

Opie, the gangling Yank, coiled himself down in a corner of one of the settees, his friendly grin inviting the small talk of those who felt like yarning. The American considered himself privileged to be in on the raid; but he, too, had begun to suffer from the tension that pervaded the carrier's company from admiral downwards. So, too, he thought, must Nelson's captains have felt on the eve of Trafalgar.

Some of the aircrews went up to the darkened flight deck. In pairs and in little groups they paced up and down, talking softly, speculating, glancing frequently up at the star-filled sky.

Maund and Patch strolled together, the tall sensitive lieutenant and the short, slight captain of Marines whose dearest wish was to become – of all things – a farmer. As they paced the gently heaving deck, bracing themselves against the increasing wind force created by the carrier's thrustful passage through the night, they discussed anything that came into their minds: subjects as far removed from the forthcoming raid as could be conceived.

'We talked about the price of pigs in China,' Maund recalled afterwards, a matter of more than passing interest to the twenty-six-year-old Patch – although the realisation of his bucolic ambition would have to wait another fifteen years. They discussed, too, the disturbing effect on the peace of mind of bachelor pilots of a recent official decision that Wrens might now clothe their shapely legs in silk stockings.

At the Air Intelligence Office observers began to congregate for a last-minute briefing and a final scrutiny of the dog-eared photographs of the enemy stronghold. The briefing this time concerned their function as navigators, focusing attention on the important task of guiding their aircraft back to the ship after the raid.

The *Illustrious*, they were told, woud be steaming at sea off the island of Cephalonia - an unmistakable landmark from the air. All that was required of them after leaving Taranto was to maintain a steady course eastwards until the dark mass of the island loomed up below. Then they must fly along its coastline to the south-east corner until they spotted the waiting carrier. But once they came within fifty miles of their mother ship they would be able to pick up her homing beacon and the rest should be easy.

Two things were not mentioned at the observers' briefing. One was that if, while they were away on the raid, the *Illustrious* should be located and engaged by enemy forces she would have to withdraw. In that event her prospects of landing-on incoming and possibly damaged aircraft would become very remote indeed.

The second was a thought that would forever remain unspoken within the hearing of the aircrews: that no one in the carrier really expected as many as half the attacking planes to return at all!

At a quarter to eight Streamline Robertson stood on his special eyrie below the compass platform, irritably scanning the illuminated dial of his wrist watch. The first strike of Swordfish ought to be readying for take-off What the hell was holding up Williamson? He despatched a messenger in search of 815's CO.

Above him Boyd, moving restlessly about the crowded bridge, cast frequent glances down at the flight deck. The wind was whipping over it now, for the carrier was steaming at twenty-eight knots. A 23,000-ton waterborne airfield speeding through the night at something over thirty miles an hour.

In fifteen minutes the *Illustrious* would reach the flying-off position, 'X for X-ray', forty miles distant from the most westerly point of Cephalonia, and 170 miles south-east of Taranto. The vast bulk of the carrier quivered and throbbed under the urgent beat of her propellers.

The minutes ticked by. Eight bells sounded faintly through the loud-speaker system, and the ship's watches changed duties. Robertson fiddled aimlessly with his green-shaded Aldis lamp as he stared down at the scene of orderly activity below the island. There had been a delay in the fuelling Williamson had told him. Now the last of the twelve Swordfish was being brought up on the foremost lift, to be wheeled aft into position by the flight deck party.

At ten minutes past eight the warning klaxons sounded. The aircrews doused their cigarettes and strolled out on to the flight deck. To some, despite the Sidcup suits and Mae Wests worn over their shirts and shorts, the wind felt chill against their bodies as they emerged from the fuggy 'tween-deck atmosphere.

Starters whirred as the fitters seated in the cockpits of the Stringbags switched on the engines.

First to board were the pilots. As each man squeezed himself into his seat the fitter stood on the opposite wing and helped him to fasten his parachute straps and Sutton harness.

The observers came last, each hefting the big canvas case that held his Bigsworth chart board, navigational instruments and binoculars. The fitters assisted them in; then, repeating a farewell gesture already made to the pilots, added a final thump on the shoulder and a shouted 'Good luck, sir,' before dropping to the deck.

For a fleeting moment as they sat, each in his small, dimly lit world, the airmen knew a sudden chill sense of loneliness; of isolation from their fellows. Then as they began automatically to busy themselves with the normalities of pre-flight routine the feeling fled.

Pilots ran up their engines, checked magnetos and oil pressure, flicked practised eyes over gauges and dials. Observers laid out chart boards and instruments, donned and adjusted the earphones of their wireless sets. Those in the torpedo planes who had to share the rear cockpit with the overload tank swore feelingly as they bumped head or elbows against this awkward neighbour.

Gosport tubes – the Swordfish's primitive form of intercom. – were plugged in, and pilots called up the men seated within a few inches of their own backs.

'You all right, old boy?'

'Yes, everything OK, Skipper.'

Bull, in the rear seat of E.4F, complained that his cockpit lighting had fused.

'Too late now, you'll have to use your torch,' decided Maund, unplugging the stethoscope-like tube. He held up a thumb, indicating 'OK for take-off', to 'Haggis' Russell, the Flight Deck

Officer, who was waiting impatiently beside his port wheel.

The fitter and rigger attending each Stringbag now lay prone on the deck, one at either side of the undercarriage, holding the wheel chocks in place. At a signal from Russell they would whisk these away, leaving the plane free to move.

As the whine of aircraft engines settled down to a steady muted roar, Russell flashed his green-shaded torch towards the lower bridge. Streamline Robertson saw it with relief, then turned and hastened up to the compass platform.

"Range ready to take off, sir,' he told Boyd.

Fabric trembling under the impelling pressure of her rudder, the carrier turned into wind. A gush of black funnel smoke plumed against the starry sky as speed was increased.

The wings of the roaring Swordfish rocked gently in the airflow of the carrier's passage, and the watchers on the flight deck gripped their caps to prevent them from being blown away. Over the loud-speakers Chaplain Lloyd began his running commentary on the take-off for the benefit of those closed up at their defence stations.

Viewed from above the pattern of the ranged Stringbags on the flight deck resembled the backbone of an outsize fish. Positioned at a forty-five degree angle to the ship's centre line, four machines were ranged to port and four to starboard. Between their angled noses four more stood in line astern.

Williamson in L.4A at the head of the centre queue kept his eyes fixed on Russell as the Flight Deck Officer placed himself on the port side, torch in hand.

Suddenly the fairy lights outlining the flight deck flicked on, and Williamson could see the steam jet spurting from the deck just beyond the foremost lift arrowing straight towards him. The ship was heading directly into wind.

Any moment now.

A green light flashed briefly from Flying Control. This was instantly followed by a horizontal sweep of Russell's torch.

'Chocks away!'

Then a circular sweep of the torch, finishing with an upward movement.

'Rev engines!'

L.4A trembled as the Bristol Pegasus thundered into full power.

A final green flash from Russell, and the Stringbag sped fleetly towards the bows. The fairy lights blurred, there was a momentary sickening drop, then abruptly Williamson and Scarlett floated in a sea of darkness. L.4A was airborne.

The time was 8.35 p.m.

Eight miles from the speeding carrier Williamson, his altimeter showing a thousand feet, dropped a flame float, then commenced to circle above it so that his range could form up on him. Red and green wingtip navigation lights were switched on as an additional beacon, and Scarlett leaned from his cockpit and began flashing the letter K with a blue-shaded torch.

In five minutes the flight deck of the *Illustrious* was clear. The first range of aircraft were safely away, climbing into the moonlit night. The fairy lights went out, and the carrier turned back on to her former course.

Away on her port hand the Swordfish laboriously manoeuvred themselves into four vics of three. Dark blue formation lights fitted to port and starboard interplane struts and on the tail helped pilots to keep in station. Maund in E.4F, peering from his cockpit, spotted his team mate Kemp in L.4K and closed up into place on his beam.

Thirteen minutes from take-off. One hundred and seventy miles to go to Taranto.

Flying at a speed of seventy-five knots, the Swordfish climbed steadily into the north-west. But no one found station-keeping easy. Williamson was forced to weave as he sought height, his heavily burdened plane seeming to claw itself bodily upwards in a series of lurches.

Spread out behind him, the rest of the Stringbags rode the air like an undisciplined school of fish; rising and falling unevenly, alternately thrusting forward, then throttling back almost to the verge of stalling, wings rocking as they caught the blast of a neighbour's slipstream.

At four thousand feet they ran into scattered cumulus, the edges of the fleecy vapour shimmering like silver gauze in the moonlight. As the altitude increased the temperature dropped.

'God, how cold it was,' wrote one pilot afterwards. 'The sort of cold that knows nothing of humanism and fills you until all else is drowned save perhaps fear and loneliness. Suspended between heaven and earth in a sort of no-man's-land. To be sure, no man was ever meant to be there – in the abyss which men of old feared to meet if they ventured to the ends of the earth. Is it surprising that my knees were knocking together?'

The cloud mass thickened, but Williamson continued to climb through it. The pilots now had their work cut out trying to maintain formation on the dim blue lights of those ahead. There was no radio-telephone in a Swordfish by means of which pilots could keep in touch; only a morse-key radio set which observers were forbidden to use on operations save for transmission in dire emergency.

Amid the murky billows of the cloud which now blanketed the moon, some of the formation became detached from the others. Maund in E.4F, after being forced to fall away to avoid collision, climbed again in pursuit of the cluster of formation lights, he could dimly glimpse above and ahead.

Ranging up at last alongside one of the swimming grey fish, an errant moonbeam illumined black figures on a fuselage to his anxious gaze. 5A -- Patch's Stringbag. E.4F climbed again in search of the torpedo-droppers.

At 7,500 feet the Swordfish at last rode clear of cloud. Williamson made a quick tally of his flock. Only eight of the Stringbags were still together.

He counted the number of torpedoes he could see gleaming between the air wheels. Five, including his own; the three other planes were the two flare-droppers and one of the bombers. The remainder must have lost touch during the climb.

He was not unduly worried about the bombers; they were due to attack independently anyhow. So long as they waited for the torpedo boys to arrive all would be well.

Time 9.15 p.m. Ninety minutes to go.

Scarlett, huddled in the cockpit behind Williamson, had uttered no word to his pilot since take-off, except to pass an occasional navigational direction. But such taciturnity was not unusual among Swordfish aircrew when on operations. Conversation through the Gosports was difficult, and observers often left the tube unplugged in order to attend to the business of navigation or to operate the wireless set.

If a pilot wished to speak to his observer and the latter had thus isolated himself, he waggled the plane wings as a calling-up signal. Similarly if a pilot had cut himself off from conversation the observer poked him in the back to attract his attention.

Suddenly Williamson saw the sky ahead of the Stringbag squadron burst into a coruscation of red, blue and orange flashes. The display rapidly increased in intensity of brilliance until it resembled an enormous cone of multi-coloured fire, rising to many thousands of feet.

Scarlett's voice now came over the Gosport, calm and unemotional. 'There's Taranto,' he said.

'Yes, and the reception committee appears to be on its toes,' Williamson commented with equal nonchalance.

The time was eight minutes to eleven.

Maund in the second sub-flight of torpedo-droppers described his first sight of Taranto as 'a mass of quaint-coloured, twinkling flashes, like liver spots,' in the sky to starboard.

A few minutes before this Bull, his observer, had confirmed that a flashing light below came from the lighthouse on Cape Santa Maria di Luca, the heel of Italy. The squadron had entered the Gulf of Taranto.

Maund reminded him to switch off the overload tank, then settle down to follow the motions of his leader.

Orbiting over the Gulf, Swayne in L.4M saw the approach of the squadron with relief. For nearly half an hour his Stringbag had been sailing alone about a hostile sky within shouting distance of Taranto awaiting their arrival. His was the torpedo-bomber which had lost touch with the squadron during that climb through cloud over the sea. Steering direct for the target area at a lower altitude, he had made better time than they.

L.4M took station astern of Kemp in L.4K.

'Shall I detach the flare-droppers?' asked Scarlett.

'Yes, please.'

The reply was as quietly polite as if Williamson had been offered a cup of tea in the wardroom of the *Illustrious*.

Scarlett twisted round in his seat and flashed the letter G for 'Go' twice in Morse with his pocket torch.

This was the pre-arranged signal for the lighting-up party to break off.

Kiggell in L.4P saw it and turned away towards the promontory of Cape San Vito. Lamb in L.5B followed him astern. He was the standby flare-dropper. If anything untoward happened to L.4P, or his flares failed to give sufficient light, Lamb would take over or reinforce the illuminations.

Spears of tracer stabbed upwards at L.4P from the enemy batteries on Cape San Vito. But the gunfire seemed to be all sound and fury. L.4P sailed unscathed on her course amid the brilliance, following the outline of the eastern shore of the harbour towards the town of Taranto itself.

'We're going to have a bumper welcome,' Kiggell had remarked to his observer as they approached the port. 'They seem to be expecting us.'

Janvrin in the rear seat, twenty-five years of age but already a married man with responsibilities, gazed at the inferno flung up by the Italian gunners and grinned mirthlessly.

'Press on regardless,' he muttered.

The first flare released by L.4P floated gracefully earthwards. It was set to burn at 4,500 feet. The time, Kiggell noted, was two minutes past eleven.

He dropped eight more flares at half-mile intervals. All burned correctly and seemed to him to be providing a satisfactory degree of illumination. He swung away to starboard, and L.5B followed him round.

Williamson pointed the nose of L.4A at the southern half of the ellipse below that was the Mar Grande, the outer harbour of Italy's premier naval base. The cone of fire was now erupting ceaselessly – a dazzling aurora of death. He thrust the stick forward, and the Stringbag began to slide down towards the fiery bowl in a shallow dive.

Speed 145 knots. Height 7,000 feet. 6,000 – 5,000 – 4,000 – 2,000 – 1,000 – 750. The altimeter needle began to race round the dial as the dive became steeper.

L.4A must make a three-and-a-half-mile run-in through the barrage, and to do this and survive she must get down almost on the deck.

Williamson watched the tracer coming at him with a morbid fascination. The red and blue balls sailed upwards so slowly – lazily almost. Then they seemed suddenly to accelerate, and literally whistled past.

He found it exciting but not unduly alarming. Like all pilots, he had an extraordinary and totally unjustifiable belief in his own personal immortality. And, since he was flying the aircraft, there was much around him to occupy his attention.

It was different for Scarlett, crouching in an unarmoured cockpit and virtually defenceless. 'For him,' Williamson wrote later, 'it must have been rather like a passenger in a car without any brakes careering down a steep hill with a learner driver at the wheel.'

Flattened out now and jinking, L.4A sped at almost mast-head height over the Digo di Tarantola.

Peering up momentarily, Scarlett saw a barrage balloon flash past one wing.

'Christ, Ken, that's bloody good flying!' he thought.

In fact, Williamson never even noticed the menace that had earlier worried him.

Ahead two Italian destroyers were shooting point-blank at

the juddering Stringbag, and for a second he was dazzled by their gun flashes. To port appeared the unmistakable outlines of an anchored battleship – one of the *Cavour* class.

He swung the Swordfish towards its bristling bulk. Spears of flame lanced at him from the warship's dark bowels.

For what seemed an eternity of time the Swordfish hung suspended in smoke-wreathed, acrid-smelling space. Then Williamson pressed the electro-magnetic torpedo release grip, and the Stringbag jerked convulsively as the 'fish' leapt from its belly.

The moment he felt the torpedo leave the plane, Williamson banked steeply to starboard. A scimitar of tracer slashed savagely at L.4A, and the Stringbag fell like a stone into the harbour.

Astern of his squadron commander, Philip Sparke in L.4C followed Williamson down to 4,000 feet, then broke away to make his own attack.

When the flame-dappled surface of the harbour was skimming past only a few feet below his wings, he lumbered across the Mar Grande like a great grey moth.

The shoal breakwater slid by beneath, then to starboard the box-like outlines of the floating dock loomed up. A few hundred yards away from it lay an Italian battleship. It was not the *Littorio*-class vessel Sparke had privately marked down as his target: it was a *Cavour*, but it would have to do, he decided.

L.4C flew straight and level towards the battleship. At seven hundred yards range Sparke released his torpedo, and wrenched the Stringbag round in a complete left-hand turn. As he roared away towards the Gulf he glanced back over his shoulder. He was in time to see a tall column of flame-shot spray leap upwards from his target. A hit!

A blast of incandescence, like the breath of Hell, buffeted L.4C as the Stringbag hurtled over the belching muzzles of the ack-ack batteries on the breakwater at the harbour entrance. Then suddenly, blessedly, shellbursts and the scorpion whips of tracer were left behind.

Calmly Neale in the rear cockpit passed over the correct course for Cephalonia, and Sparke lifted L.4C gently into the night.

Not far behind came Macauley in L.4R. Third of the trio who between them comprised the southern prong of Williamson's pincer attack on the enemy anchorage, he, too, had selected the easterly moored *Cavour* as his target.

At six hundred yards range he had dropped his 'fish' and saw it start to run, then turned and raced seawards over the Tarantola mole.

As he went the sudden recollection of menace ahead came to Macauley, a gay and uninhibited warrior.

'Where's that bloody balloon barrage?' he enquired over the Gosport of Tony Wray.

'We've been through it once,' came the resigned reply, 'and we're just going through it again!'

But, like Williamson on the run-in, Macauley caught no glimpse of the snaking steel cables which could have sliced through the Swordfish like a wire through cheese.

Clawing for height, L.4R heaved herself over the hump of Cape San Vito and was swallowed up in the darkness.

Kemp in L.4K, leading the second sub-flight which formed the northern jaw of the pincers, skirted the harbour to the westward, then came in over the western breakwater at four thousand feet.

During his glide down he was enfiladed at almost point-blank range by enemy batteries from the north and south which were spaced less than three thousand yards apart. Away on his port hand guns blazed at him from Cape Rondinella on the mainland. To starboard a battery firing from the most northerly point of San Pietro Island had him in their sights.

More hazards lay ahead in the shape of gun batteries lining the nothern shore of the mainland, and a pair of ack-ack ships secured to buoys a few hundred yards inside the breakwater. Then came a fence of barrage balloons suspended from dumb lighters and, anchored within the haven of a rectangle of hanging torpedo nets, three large cruisers. To port was Taranto Island, bristling with guns.

Silhouetted against the wan light of Kiggell's leisurely descending flares, Kemp could see the enemy battleships. They lay in a wide arc spaced about six hundred yards apart: two *Cavours* to the north; two *Littorio's*, then two more *Cavours*. He marked down the most northerly of the larger battleships as his prey.

Diving steeply, L.4K whistled through the gap between Taranto Island and the nearest cruiser. Multi-coloured tracer from the warship's close-range AA weapons and orange flashes from her larger guns lashed out at the flying Stringbag. Gunfire also came spouting up from a cluster of small merchant vessels lying close inshore.

Kemp had time to notice with a grin of vindictive satisfaction that, due to the low elevation at which her guns were firing, shells from the nearest cruiser were slamming into the unhappy merchantmen.

Then, as if to allow the intruder breathing space in which to perform the act for which he had entered the arena, the cruisers suddenly ceased fire.

Winging across the water at nought feet, like some great ungainly insect, L.4K aimed her nose directly at the *Littorio* battleship.

When he judged that the rapidly shrinking distance between plane and warship had dropped to a thousand yards, Kemp's hand closed tightly on the torpedo release grip.

Leaning out of his cockpit, Bailey stared down at the water with straining eyes until the bubbling track of the 'fish' appeared streaking towards its huge target.

Then, as if in lethal applause, the guns of the nearby cruisers once more belched flame and thunder.

Kemp climbed steeply to starboard, lifting L.4K clear of the mole and its sentinel balloons. As he fled southwards he snatched a backward glance and saw flames shoot up from the seaplane sheds away to the north-east. The bomber boys were on the job.

Meanwhile Swayne in L.4M had charged in over the western breakwater at a thousand feet. The batteries to north and south were firing wildly in all directions, but most of their shells and bullets whizzed harmlessly over the careering Stringbag.

'Why the hell aren't they using searchlights?' wondered Swayne.

If the defenders had in fact done so it is possible that not one of the Swordfish would have survived even to reach a target, much less escape. But the extraordinary fact is that although searchlights formed an integral part of the Taranto defences, the Italians did not use them on the night of November 11th.

Losing height rapidly, Swayne tore across the Mar Grande. When the thin grey line of the eastern shoal breakwater showed up beneath his wings, he turned sharply to port so as to dive on to the northerly *Littorio* from the south-east.

Almost at the same moment as Kemp fired his torpedo from the northward, Swayne let go his 'fish' at a range of four hundred yards. Then, unaware of L.4K hurtling southwards above him, him, Swayne heaved his Stringbag up and over the battleship herself. As they flashed between the steel masts Buscall, peering from the rear cockpit, thought he saw a column of smoke soar up from the decks below.

Banking to port, Swayne now streaked back across the Mar Grande, pursued by a stream of badly aimed fire from the cruisers. To the bemused Italian sailors the harbour seemed to be full of diving Swordfish.

San Pietro Island erupted afresh as Swayne whistled overhead. But the gunners had no time to pinpoint their enemy, and L.4M disappeared unscathed into the blackness above the Gulf.

Maund in E.4F, last of this first strike of torpedo-droppers came in over Rondinella Point and glided down towards the north-west corner of the harbour. He followed the curve of the northern shoreline, and at a height of a thousand feet passed over the town of Taranto itself, a neat patchwork of houses and gardens.

So far his approach remained undetected. Then the sound locators of a Breda gun battery picked up the drone of his engine, and red tracer soared up angrily. Other guns joined in.

Coolly Maund came down to a hundred feet and checked his position with the aid of a factory chimney he could see in the distance. Then he let the Swordfish down still further and began his dash over the water.

All hell broke loose as the cruisers' gunners and those manning the canal batteries spotted the jinking Stringbag.

Scudding along just above the surface of the harbour, so low that Maund wondered if they would hit the sea before they could let go their torpedo, he sighted the distant shapes of two battleships ahead. The second vessel, her outlines darkly etched against the silvery background of the flares, was the larger. She must be a *Littorio* and therefore a more worthwhile target.

At thirteen hundred yards Maund pressed the tit, and E.4F lifted as the torpedo dived away. Bull, watching anxiously for the track, saw the creamy bubbles appear and experienced a great wave of relief. Now for the getaway.

Turning sharply to starboard, Maund took E.4F towards the commercial basin, and for several breathless moments dodged nimbly in and out among the clustered merchantmen.

Suddenly he found himself almost on top of an Italian destroyer. For one heart-stopping second he gazed down the muzzle of a pom-pom gun. To Maund it loomed as large as a 15-inch. Yet, incredulously, the gunners did not fire.

Throttle wide open, E.4F fled away, turning and twisting like a trapped animal frantically seeking a way of escape.

A stream of fire lashed out from the cruisers, the tracers streaking past so close to the Stringbag's cockpit that Maund could smell the acrid smoke. San Pietro Island loomed up below, then was gone, leaving only the tearing sound of bursting shells.

Zigzagging wildly, Maund found that he had reached the open sea. Then as he sent the Swordfish soaring aloft he stared back with unbelieving eyes at the hell from which they had emerged.

'My Christ, Bull,' he yelled half hysterically over the Gosport, 'just look at that bloody awful mess – look at it! Just look at it!'

Around them the air felt cool and peaceful. A handful of floating clouds cast dark shadows on the moonlit sea below. E.4F climbed above them, then steadied on a course due east.

Four minutes after Kiggell released his first flare and Williamson was positioning himself for his run-in, Ollie Patch in Swordfish E.5A sailed over San Pietro Island at 8,500 feet. His task was to dive-bomb the enemy cruisers and destroyers which, he had been told, were berthed stern-on to the jetties at the south shore of the Mar Piccolo.

Unemotionally Patch glanced at what he afterwards described as 'the wonderful Brock's display' as E.5A crossed the four-mile width of the Mar Grande. From time to time shell-bursts rocked the Stringbag but she was not hit.

As they neared the Mar Piccolo the barrage grew more fierce. The nests of gun batteries on Taranto Island and around the naval base flung up a curtain of steel with hysterical abandon.

At first neither Patch nor Goodwin could see their target. Due to the angle of declination of the moon the whole of the southern shore of the inner harbour lay in shadow. The darkness here seemed to be intensified rather than lessened by the flares which hung suspended in the eastern sky.

After scouting round for two minutes, which seemed more like hours, Patch spotted the ships at last. Two of the Italian cruisers lay moored to buoys in the centre of the Mar Piccolo. The remainder were berthed alongside pens which jutted out at right angles to the main quay.

All the ships were adding their own quota of gunfire to the deafening bedlam. But to Patch there was nothing personal about the enemy shooting. Without searchlights to hold the attackers in their revealing beams, the gunners were firing more or less blindly at aircraft they could hear but not see.

He took E.5A round to the northwest, banked steeply, and from a height of only fifteen hundred feet dived down over the line of anchored vessels.

When the Swordfish was down to almost masthead level Patch flattened out and pressed the bomb-release button. Curving away in succession the six bombs, three from each wing rack, and one pair of Marine's part-worn marching boots whistled downwards.

Pom-pom shells hosed briefly at the Stringbag as it flashed across a gun position on the quay, but again the miracle held and the gunners scored no hits. Patch edged the stick over to port and E.5A sped eastward from the fiery hell that was Taranto.

Muttering a heartfelt 'Thank God, that's over,' Goodwin turned to see what damage their bombs had wreaked. But all he saw was what Kemp in L.4K had already spotted as he fled away to the southward: the seaplane station to the east of the naval base wreathed in flames and blazing merrily.

Ten minutes later while they were hedge-hopping over the peaceful Italian countryside at fifty feet, Patch and Goodwin were rudely reminded that this was hostile territory. A cluster of peasants' cottages had just shown up whitely in the moonlight below when without warning a rapid stream of tracer fire fountained up at them.

Patch weaved violently, then dived the Swordfish for cover behind a nearby range of hills.

'The saucy so-and-so's!' muttered Goodwin indignantly.

Eight miles from Taranto E.5A crossed the coast and headed out towards Greece.

Sarra in L.4L was the pilot responsible for the blaze in the seaplane base. Coming in at 8,000 feet over the western mainland and diving to fifteen hundred feet above the Mar Piccolo, he, like Patch, had been unable to pick out his assigned target.

He had passed over the shadowy dockyard and was flying along the southern shore of the inner harbour when he suddenly spotted the hangars and slipways of the seaplane base ahead. At once he decided that this would make an excellent alternative.

Sarra knew that the place was defended by several batteries of close-range AA weapons, but he hoped that the gun crews would be too engrossed in admiring the dazzling display of pyrotechnics taking place over the Mar Grande to notice his approach until it was too late.

Swooping out of the sky like a great bat, the pilot let go his stick of bombs at five hundred feet. He saw one of the 250-pounders plunge through the roof of a hangar, its arrival inside being immediately followed by a heavy explosion. Other bombs blossomed redly on the slipways.

The enemy batteries sprang into belated life, some of the pom-pom and machine-gun fire being particularly intense. But Sarra was not disposed to hang about. He pointed the nose of L.4L to the south-east and went hell for leather towards the coast.

Last of the bombers was Tony Forde in L.4H, who arrived over the harbour just as Kiggell dropped the first flare. He had lost touch with Patch, the bomber leader, during the earlier mix-up in the clouds and decided to remain with Williamson's party.

While the torpedo-bombers were lining up for their run-in, Forde headed unmolested across country over Cape San Vito and the low ground to the east of the town of Taranto. He reached the eastern end of the Mar Piccolo just as Sarra was circling over the dockyard in search of his target.

Since he was flying with his back to the glare above the Mar Grande, Forde had much less difficulty in identifying the anchored ships in their pens. Peering down from his cockpit, they looked to him like a row of sardines in a tin. He passed over the northern shore of the inner harbour, then turned and dived south-westward on to his prey.

At fifteen hundred feet Forde levelled off and let go his bombs. The first of these hit the water a few yards short of the nearer of two cruisers moored side by side against the quay. The rest of the stick ought to have landed squarely on the target, he felt; but neither he nor Mardel-Ferreira who was craning from the back seat, saw the hoped-for hits.

Uncertain now whether the remainder of the bombs had in fact released properly, Forde took L.4H round the western basin of the Mar Piccolo, then calmly repeated the attack.

During this entire manoeuvre L.4H was pursued by intense anti-aircraft fire from the two cruisers moored in the centre of the harbour. Yet once more the amazing luck of the attackers held, and the Stringbag was not hit by a single bullet or shell splinter.

Deciding that two bites at the cherry were more than enough, Forde now spurted away to the north-west, and crossed the coast five miles from the harbour. His last glimpse of the Mar

Piccolo was the brightly flowering explosion of Sarra's bomb hit on the seaplane hangar.

Meanwhile Kiggell and Janvrin in L.4P, after dropping their flares successfully, cruised around the eastern perimeter of the Mar Grande watching the start of the torpedo attack. Astern of them Lamb and Grieve in L.5B similarly enjoyed a grand-stand view of the great assault. Then both Stringbags went down in succession after their own target.

This was the oil storage depot behind Cape San Vito from which a pipeline ran to an oiling jetty at the south-eastern corner of the harbour. One after the other the Swordfish pilots pointed the noses of their machines at the oil tanks and dived at a steep angle.

Flattening out at fifteen hundred feet, they let go their bombs. But, disappointingly, they saw no results Then both turned and streaked away southwards, pursued by streams of wildly aimed flak from the storage depot's guardian battery.

The first raid was over. From start to finish it had lasted for twenty-three minutes.

CHAPTER IX

THE SECOND STRIKE

WHILE Williamson and his men were climbing through the cloud layer on their way to Taranto, the *Illustrious* and her escorts, cruising at seventeen knots, had swept round in a thirty-mile circle, and were once more approaching position 'X for X-ray'. Aft on the carrier's flight deck the second strike of nine Swordfish had already been ranged for take-off.

Hale, with Lieutenant 'Georgie' Carline as his observer and master navigator, was to lead his reduced squadron in Swordfish L.5A. The four other torpedo-bombers were Lieutenant Charles Lea in L.5H, with Sub-Lieutenant 'Johnna' Jones as observer; 'Tiffy' Torrens-Spence in L.5K with Alfie Sutton in the rear seat; Gerry Bayly and 'Tod' Slaughter in E.4H; and John Wellham of Bomba Gulf fame, with Lieutenant Pat Humphreys as observer, in E.5H.

Flare-droppers for the strike were Lieutenant Dick Hamilton and Sub-Lieutenant Weekes in L.5B; and Lieutenant Ronald Skelton with Sub-Lieutenant Edgar Perkins of the RNVR, in L.4F. Clifford and Going in L.5F; and Lieutenant Sam Morford and Sub-Lieutenant Raymond Green in L.5Q, comprised the tiny bomber force.

As before, the flare-droppers also carried four bombs apiece with which to add to the general confusion after they had performed their principal task of lighting the way for the torpedo planes.

While the carrier worked up speed and they waited to be called out on to the flight deck, Hale and his team mates mulled over their chances of survival. On balance it seemed that Williamson and his men would be the luckier since they could at least hope to achieve surprise. But by the time the second party arrived over the target area Taranto would undoubtedly be buzzing like a nest of angry hornets.

'Let's hope the Ities run out of ammo before we get there,' prayed Lea fervently.

At 9.20 p.m., Boyd turned the *Illustrious* into wind, and the second fly-off began.

First away, Hale flew to a position off the port bow, as Williamson had done before him, dropped a flame float and commenced to circle round it while he waited for his team to form up on him.

In rapid succession six of the Stringbags followed him into the air. Then the accident happened.

The Swordfish had been ranged in the customary herring-bone pattern on either side of the after-end of the flight deck. Take-off was effected by bringing the aircraft forward from port and starboard sides alternately. Since flying-off was always a split-second evolution, each machine as it taxied to the centre of the flight deck was at once followed by the next in line from the opposite side.

Last but one of the strike, Clifford in L.5F had just begun to move into the centre position when Morford in L.5Q also started to taxi forward from his place on the port side. But someone misjudged the distance between them, and the Stringbags met and locked wings together.

When 'Haggis' Russell saw what had happened he ran forward and flashed the signal for both pilots to cut engines. Fitters and riggers came racing up, and the two Stringbags were disentangled and carefully examined.

Morford's aircraft appeared to have suffered no injury, but some of the fabric had been ripped off the mainplane of L.5F and several of the wing ribs were broken.

'God damn it to hell!' raged Going when he saw the damage. 'After all the bloody trouble I've been through today this has to happen!'

Russell ran across to report the mishap to Robertson in Flying Control, and 'Streamline' hastened up to the compass platform to tell Boyd that two of the Swordfish were out of action.

'I don't think we'd better go on then,' decided the carrier captain. 'The seven already off will have to do the best they can.'

'I'm pretty sure Morford can still get away, sir,' Robertson told him, 'but Clifford's machine will have to be struck down for repairs.'

'All right. Get Morford up then,' ordered Boyd.

A few minutes later L.5Q took off smoothly, her departure watched with tightened lips by the furious Going. Clifford, his pilot, had vanished with their damaged aircraft to the hangar below to see what could be done to make her fit to fly.

Ten minutes after the waiting Hale had been joined by L.5Q the strike leader began to wonder what had happened to the ninth member of the party. At last, after another five minutes had elapsed a signal lamp on the bridge of the distant carrier winked at the circling Stringbags.

Carline read the Morse to Hale over the Gosport. The message consisted of two words only, 'Carry on'.

Hale, who knew how keen Going was to take part in the raid, shook his head regretfully. Poor old Grubby, he thought. Still, perhaps it was as well that he couldn't make it. After his crash that morning this certainly did not seem to be his lucky day.

With his torch Carline signalled the range to assume flight formation. Then in three vics, the last one incomplete, the Stringbags climbed away to the north-west.

The time was 9.45 p.m.

Pollock and Opie were alone in the AIO when the door was flung open to admit Going, who slammed his instrument bag viciously on to the nearest chair.

'Of all the blasted bad luck,' snarled the observer, 'why can't they give us a chance to get off?' His voice rose as he ranted on.

'Look,' said Opie kindly when he could get a word in, 'it's no good moaning to us about it. If you want to change things why don't you go and see the captain?'

Going gnawed his lip. 'I can't possibly do that,' he said.

'Why not?' asked Pollock. 'He's very human. Go and see him,' he added persuasively.

For a long moment Going considered the suggestion.

'By God, I believe I will,' he muttered.

Impulsively he dashed out and buttonholed Robertson on the flying-control platform.

'Sir,' he begged, 'can't we take off as soon as the damage to our kite is patched up? I'm sure it won't take very long.'

Streamline shook his head. 'No, it's too late,' he decided.

'Well, then, may I see the captain about it?' urged Going desperately.

Robertson shrugged. 'All right,' he said, and led the way up to the compass platform.

Boyd listened silently to the airman's eloquent pleading. Then without a word he went over to consult with Lyster, a hunched figure in a corner of the bridge. In a few moments he returned.

'Do you think you can catch up with the others?' he asked Going.

'Yes, sir, I think we can,' stammered Grubby, realising as he spoke that such a thing was almost palpably impossible.

'Very well,' said Boyd. 'I'll give you ten minutes.'

It was in fact twenty-four minutes after Hale and his eight Swordfish had departed that the *Illustrious* once more turned into wind. At 9.58 p.m., the sweating riggers who had been working at top speed to restore L.5F to a serviceable condition stood on the flight deck and watched the solitary Stringbag lurch off the end of the bows and vanish into the night.

'Blimey, they've got more guts than I have,' commented one of the riggers to his mate, as the fairy lights went out and the carrier turned back on course.

Clifford and Going knew nothing about it until after the raid, but the other participant in the ill-fated collision was now about to run into misfortune.

At five minutes past ten, one of the two metal straps securing the long-range fuel tank to the underside of the fuselage of Swordfish L.5Q snapped. For an instant the heavy tank hung suspended by the second strap, petrol siphoning away in a fine spray. Then the remaining strap gave way, and the tank hurtled down into the sea below.

At the same moment L.5Q's engine cut out, and the Swordfish spun away out of control.

When the accident happened the flight was cruising at three thousand feet, just beneath the cloud base which had been steadily spreading until it now covered the sky. Hale saw L.5Q go spiralling down, and watched until the Stringbag vanished from his view.

'Hell,' he thought, 'poor old Morford's had it now.'

For a moment he debated whether to report the mishap to the *Illustrious*. But the success of the night's operation was far more important than the fate of one aircraft, and he decided against breaking wireless silence. Morford and Green would have to fend for themselves.

Meanwhile, after falling helplessly for nearly a thousand feet, Morford at last managed to regain control and level out. But the broken tank straps now began to drum against the fuselage with a most alarming clatter. Neither Morford nor Green realised immediately what was causing this devil's tattoo. At any second it seemed as if the fabric would split asunder and the aircraft fold up in mid-air.

It was manifestly impossible to continue the flight in this condition. Accordingly Morford carefully nursed L.5Q around in a wide circle, and they started back to the carrier.

He knew that their approach would be picked up on the ship's radar, and he hoped that Schierbeck would exercise his wizardry and come to the correct conclusion as to the identity of the blip on his scan. For, although Morford would have been justified in using his radio to acquaint the *Illustrious* with his plight, he, too, decided that the risk of giving away the ship's position to the enemy was too great.

As soon as they sighted the carrier and her attendant warships below in the moonlight, Green fired a red Very cartridge as a distress signal. But the gunners of the *Illustrious* and her consorts were taking no chances, and at once opened fire on the limping Swordfish. After all, this could be an Italian snooper.

Morford hastily took L.5Q out of gun range, and Green leaned from his cockpit and fired a two-star identification signal. To the relief of the airmen the gunfire then ceased. But even now Morford felt doubtful of their reception and for a further fifteen minutes he continued to circle out of gun range.

At last, however, he decided that the trigger-happy gunners must be satisfied as to their identity. He made another cautious approach, and this time was landed on without hindrance.

As Morford heaved himself out of the cockpit and climbed down on to the flight deck he turned to Russell and Robertson who had arrived to inspect the damage.

'That, sirs,' he remarked reproachfully, 'was not a very warm welcome!'

By 10.50 p.m., the sky above Hale and his six companions had cleared of cloud, and the formation began to climb to operational height. Twenty minutes later they sited a greenish-coloured cone of fire in the sky a long way off. It was Taranto, sixty miles away.

'Look at that, Georgie,' commented Hale to Carline. 'Ken Williamson must have caused a hell of a lot of damage for all that stuff to be going up.'

'Well, at least we know exactly where we've got to go,' chuckled Carline. 'That'll save wear and tear on the navigators.'

'Tiffy' Torrens-Spence in L.5K gazed at the distant fountain of flak with awe. Although by no means a pessimist, the sight of this now firmly convinced him that once they came within its range they must all inevitably be shot down.

Seated behind him, Alfie Sutton, who, by slightly mistuning his radio, had been enjoying an Italian opera broadcast, stared at the sinister glow in the heavens and felt a chill of fear run up his spine. If only he could wake up in bed with his wife and find that this was all a bad dream!

Below and to starboard flashed the beams of the lighthouse on Cape Santa Maria di Luca. Carline took a fix on this landmark. A few minutes later the range entered the Gulf of Taranto, keeping a distance of fifteen miles off shore.

But if the Italians had no effective radar they possessed some excellent sound locators, and a number of enemy coastal batteries hopefully opened fire on the approaching planes.

The shellbursts were too far off to worry the raiders, and they flew steadily on until the north-western coast of the Gulf came in view. It was then ten minutes to midnight.

Flying at eight thousand feet, the squadron now turned north-east. Five minutes after they altered course Hale ordered the flare-droppers to break off.

As soon as he saw the flash of Carline's torch, Hamilton in L.5B turned away towards Cape San Vito, closely followed by Skelton in L.4F. During the squadron's approach the gunfire from the harbour defences had died down. But now as the two flare-dropping Swordfish skimmed over the eastern shore of the Mar Grande, the Italian batteries once more opened up a furious cannonade.

Maintaining a height of five thousand feet, Hamilton sailed round the perimeter of the harbour, methodically dropping flares at fifteen-second intervals. All sixteen burned successfully, and Skelton reinforced their illumination by shedding eight more to the south-east.

Then, attacking in succession from different angles, the two Stringbags dived on to the oil storage depot.

Hamilton saw his bombs go in and flames shoot up. Skelton observed no results at all from his own attack, and concluded that his bombs had missed. The Italian gunners were also out of luck, although some of their shellbursts came uncomfortably close to L.4F. The flare-droppers pulled out of their dives and made for the coast like bats out of hell.

In the meantime the five torpedo-bombers, now high to the north-west of the harbour, assumed line astern formation. In order to fox the enemy sound locators Hale led his Stringbags across the coast and back again. On the second approach he flicked his formation lights briefly on and off in the prearranged signal for attack, and went down in a long shallow dive.

It was then that the presence of Clifford and Morford to create their planned diversion over the inner harbour would have been most welcome. With nothing to distract their attention now that the flare-droppers had made their precipitate departure, the Italian gunners were able to concentrate on the approaching torpedo planes.

Wrote Sutton afterwards: 'I gazed down upon a twinkling mass of orange-red lights which I knew was a solid curtain of bursting shells through which we had to fly. It looked absolutely terrifying.'

It was terrifying.

Unable to see their foes, the Italians threw up a box barrage of colossal intensity. All guns that would bear, ashore and afloat, were firing upwards at a predetermined range and deflection, so that every foot of the sky above the harbour seemed to be filled with stabbing points of flame. The air quivered and shook under the ceaseless detonations.

Hale's approach had brought the Stringbags over the western shore of the Mar Grande in an almost direct north-south line. Beneath them as they glided down lay the commercial basin bristling with anti-aircraft guns. To port the enemy cruisers and destroyers in the Mar Piccolo could keep them in their gun-sights for most of the way down. To starboard they could be enfiladed by ack-ack batteries on the northern shore and the guns on San Pietro Island. Directly ahead lay the worst hazard of all. For the Stringbags would have to fly straight on to the guns of the battleships themselves. Beyond the ships hung the menacing curtain of the enemy balloon barrage.

As Swordfish L.5A began her dive Hale squinted through the whirling propeller at the flak streaming past. Red, white and green balls of tracer floated by as if on an endless belt. He jinked the Stringbag violently from side to side in an effort to avoid them. But still they came at him until it seemed that the Swordfish was sliding down a chute of multi-coloured fire.

Yet, oddly enough, he could hear nothing of the bedlam around him; only the full-throated roar of the Stringbag's engine. Although the diving plane bucked and reared continuously under the concussion of bursting shells, to the pilot she felt as steady as a rock. But the acrid reek of explosives filled his nostrils and caught at his throat.

A glance at the altimeter told Hale that the Stringbag was now down to a thousand feet. He must lose as much height as possible for the torpedo run.

Through the murk ahead he could make out the shape of a *Cavour*-class battleship, with another of the same class just beyond. But a few degrees to starboard of the second vessel loomed the monstrous silhouette of a *Littorio*. She was his target.

At thirty feet Hale flattened out and winged towards the giant battleship like a moth at a candle.

As the shimmering, flame-streaked water raced past below, Hale gripped the control column with one hand while with the other he fumbled for the torpedo release button. Behind him Carline stared fixedly at the battleship which seemed to be swelling visibly every second until they appeared to be rushing straight at a massive steel cliff.

At seven hundred yards range Hale released the torpedo. Then, as he felt the sudden lightening of weight, he banked sharply to starboard and streaked away towards the harbour mouth. Tracer stabbed viciously at the rocketing Swordfish from every side.

As L.5A flashed past the end of the Tarantola mole, Carline glanced up and saw the glistening shapes of a line of barrage balloons. At the same moment Hale spotted a lighter in the water below. Automatically he skirted the obstruction without realising that a steel cable anchoring one of the balloons snaked up from the vessel's deck.

The last barrier had been passed. Only a lucky shot could harm them now.

Still keeping low above the water, L.5A tore along in the shadow of Cape San Vito. Then Hale lifted her over the line of foam marking the shoal breakwater at the harbour entrance.

A machine gun from somewhere to starboard spat a brief valediction in the shape of a whiplash of red tracer. Then, as if a door had been slammed behind them, the noise and glare were suddenly extinguished, and the Stringbag soared into the moonlight.

Carline's voice came over the Gosport. 'Good show, Ginge,' he said. 'Course one-three-five.'

Third in the line of diving Swordfish came Lea and Jones in L.5H. Tall, fair-haired and blue-eyed, Lea rejoiced in the sobriquet of 'The Colonel'. He was a first -class pilot.

Jones, his observer, was known to all as 'the imperturbable'. Together they made an excellent team.

As Lea's Stringbag came sailing down over Cape Rondinella, fountains of accurately aimed flak rose to greet him. But he had no intention of allowing L.5H to become an Aunt Sally for the enemy gunners. They ought to have used up all their ammunition by now, he thought crossly.

He executed a smart right-hand turn and followed this by going round in a complete circle, losing height rapidly. These manoeuvres brought the Stringbag beneath the soaring shell-bursts, and Lea gained a short breathing space which enabled him to glance round the target area.

He noted that the gunfire streaming up from the cruisers to his right and the ships and shore batteries away to the left met in a protective cone above the Italian battleships. Lea decided to move in under this fiery umbrella.

At a low altitude he trundled round the curve of the northern shoreline, then turned south-east. There before him lay the finest target he had ever seen. It was a *Cavour*-class battleship offering a perfect beam shot.

Flying at barely twenty feet above the surface of the harbour, Lea took L.5H in like an arrow. At eight hundred yards he loosed his torpedo.

'Give the boy a clay pipe!' he grinned exultantly, for his 'fish' could not possibly miss.

A split second after he had pressed the tit Lea banked steeply to starboard. He was about to straighten out when a swift glance ahead revealed the mast of an anchored fishing smack rushing towards him. Instinctively he jerked the stick over, and the mast whipped by with barely an inch to spare.

The new course took the straining Swordfish between two of the steadily firing cruisers anchored to the west of the battleships. Throttle wide open, L.5H roared above one of the Italian ships with so little clearance that the blast of her guns almost lifted Lea out of his seat.

'Christ!' he thought, 'I'll bet the undercart's gone for a Burton.'

But this was neither the time nor place to have a look. Still maintaining a height of less than thirty feet he drove on, and fled across the northern tip of San Pietro Island into the darkness beyond.

As the uproar faded astern Lea turned in his seat and looked back. A glowing red ball which was rapidly becoming larger and larger met his astonished gaze. With a sudden shock he realised that it was a 'flaming onion' coming straight at him!

He jammed the stick forward and L.5H almost stood on her nose. As she dipped the pursuing shell whizzed overhead, struck the sea with a hiss and bounced away into the night.

Lea drew a breath of relief and began slowly to gain height.

It was only then that he remembered his observer. It seemed hours since they had spoken over the Gosport. He plugged in the tube.

'You all right, Johnna?' he asked anxiously.

His worried frown dissolved into an admiring grin as he listened to the calm reply.

'Yes, thanks,' drawled Jones, the imperturbable. 'Hang on a minute and I'll give you the course back to the ship.'

Their last sight of the flaming inferno that was Taranto was a tall column of black smoke billowing from the centre of the Mar Grande. Could be that one of the boys had been unlucky and that smoke was funeral pyre.

Torrens-Spence in L.5K followed Lea over Cape Rondinella and at once put his Stringbag into a steep dive. His intention was to level out some five hundred yards south of the canal connecting the inner and outer harbours. From then on a short run would suffice to bring them within torpedo range of the most northerly of the four *Cavour*-class battleships.

'Down, down we went in that screaming, whistling torpedo dive,' recorded Sutton. 'All the enemy close-range weapons had now opened fire. We could see multiple batteries by the entrance to the inner harbour pouring stuff out right next to our dropping position. Tracer and incendiaries and horrible things we called "flaming onions" came streaming up at us.'

Then, to the horror of pilot and observer, another Swordfish suddenly appeared in their headlong path. The newcomer was weaving frantically from side to side in an endeavour to shake off the clawing spears of tracer.

Drastic avoiding action was necessary to avert a collision, and Torrens-Spence acted instinctively. With a swift thrust of the control column he sent L.5K spinning below the intruder. As they whipped beneath the other machine Sutton caught a glimpse of a bright orange flash above him, and from the tail of his eye saw the aircraft fall away out of control.

Neither man knew until later that they had witnessed the last surviving moments of Swordfish E.4H. Bayly's premonition had been right after all. Neither he nor Slaughter, his observer, were ever seen alive again.

But amid that whirling maelstrom of fire and death there could be no thought for the fate of others. This was an operation without parallel in their experience: its survival must be literally a case of every man for himself.

L.5K plunged out of the shell-torn sky immediately above the Italian cruisers anchored in the centre of the Mar Grande. With a stomach-jolting wrench Torrens-Spence pulled out of the dive at masthead level. Almost in the same instant the cruiser gunners saw the Stringbag and opened fire. Seeming to move along tracks of dazzling tracer, L.5K skidded across the battleship anchorage.

Amid the bewildering array of masts, funnels and bristling gun turrets surrounding them there was barely a split second in which to choose a target.

'The one to port is too close,' shouted Torrens-Spence. 'What's that ahead?'

'That's a *Littorio*,' yelled Sutton.

'Right, she's our meat, then,' decided the tall pilot, and drove L.5K directly at the giant battleship.

'She saw us and opened fire,' wrote Sutton. 'The flash of her close-range weapons stabbed at us first one and then another along her length opened up. We were coming in on her beam, and we were the centre of an incredible mass of crossfire from the cruisers and battleships and shore batteries. No worries about clear range or gun zones for the Italians. They just fired every thing they had except the 15-inch, and I could see the shots from the battleships bursting among the cruisers and merchant ships. The place stank of cordite and incendiaries and was wreathed in smoke.'

At seven hundred yards Torrens-Spence pressed the torpedo release grip.

Nothing happened!

By now the immense bulk of the *Littorio* seemed to fill their entire vision. At any moment the juddering Swordfish must surely be blown to fragments.

Feverishly Torrens-Spence recocked the release grip, then pressed again.

This time he felt L.5K lift as the torpedo dived away, and immediately spun the Stringbag round in a steep right-hand turn. As he straightened out to begin the getaway run there came a sudden jarring shock, and a tall column of water fountained in the wake of the hurtling Swordfish.

'We're hit! We're down!'

Sutton could have sworn he yelled the words aloud. But in fact he uttered no sound.

Nor had L.5K been hit, although she was now racing through an avenue of gunfire spouting from the battleships on one side and the moored cruisers on the other. Torrens-Spence had come down so low that L.5K's undercarriage had hit the water, and her air wheels were now actually skimming the surface.

Ahead of the speeding Swordfish a pair of barrage balloons hung pendant, vast glistening spheres in the lurid glow of the harbour. The lighters to which they were moored were spaced less than four hundred yards apart.

But from the moment they started their dive upon the enemy harbour Torrens-Spence had become the dedicated, icily cool airman, indifferent to everything but the task in hand. With consummate skill he sent L.5K zigzagging along that fiery corridor, out between the guardian lighters and into the darkness beyond.

There was now more than a mile to go to the harbour mouth. But the enemy gunners in the anchorage could no longer see them, and their passage over the shoal water was undisputed.

Suddenly two dark shapes loomed up in the water below.

They must be warships guarding the harbour entrance, but there had been no sign of these on the reconnaissance photographs. Now L.5K was charging down on them at more than a hundred miles an hour.

There was no chance of turning away without being seen. The enemy gunners must already have spotted the Swordfish winging along the path of the moon towards them.

Torrens-Spence jerked back on the stick, and the Stringbag rose abruptly like a rocketing pheasant. As she soared overhead the guardships erupted into flame beneath, and the airmen felt the searing gunblast like a hot breath on their goggled faces.

Alerted by this sudden activity under their noses, the batteries on Cape San Vito and San Paolo Island joined in and, as Sutton laconically commented, 'the whole merry party started up again.'

But except for a bullet hole through the fuselage, L.5K got away unscathed.

While his team mates were following one another down through the flak-filled sky over the Mar Grande, Wellham in E.5H came in more to the eastward of Cape Rondinella.

He passed above the Mar Piccolo and the town of Taranto, then altered course to starboard and made for the centre of the outer anchorage. Thus he crossed astern of the three enemy cruisers lying within the sanctuary of their anti-torpedo nets.

The whole area was carpeted with gunflashes and bursting shells, shot through with dazzling ribbons of tracer. It was a prodigal waste of ammunition, but to the Italian gunners enemy aircraft seemed to be diving on them from every side, and they fired blindly at anything that moved, real or imaginary.

Wellham's passage to the middle of the harbour was unseen and unopposed, and he was able to mark the position of the enemy battleships away on his left. They were so clearly visible in the moonlight that Skelton's flares, slowly descending in the sky beyond them, seemed unnecessary.

He banked steeply to port and commenced to glide down in preparation for his torpedo run. Suddenly the amorphous bulk of a barrage balloon loomed up ahead. To Wellham's straining gaze the thing looked as big as the dome of St. Paul's. Hands and feet clamped instantly on stick and rudder bar, and E.5H swished past the big gasbag with barely inches to spare.

A moment later the Swordfish staggered under the impact of a stream of machine-gun fire. One of the bullets struck an outer aileron, and with Wellham fighting to retain control, the Stringbag came sideslipping down on to the fiercely firing battleships.

If he could manage to flatten out in time, the course of E.5H would take her directly between the two huge *Littorios*, which lay almost abreast each other with barely half a mile separating them. Since both vessels appeared to be moored with their bows pointing to mid-harbour, Wellham would have no chance of a beam torpedo shot at either.

Astern of each of the big ships a smaller *Cavour* was anchored. All four thus appeared to be lying at the corners of a huge square. Beyond them rose the shoreline and, suspended in a semi-circle above it, a long row of barrage balloons.

Wellham, now once more in control of the plunging Swordfish, was faced with the necessity of making a lightning decision.

If he took his Stringbag between all four of the battleships he might survive long enough to be able to turn, level out and fire a beam shot at one of the *Cavours*. On the other hand he might be blasted out of the sky before he even reached the leading vessels.

The alternative was to risk an angled shot at the most southerly of the *Littorios* lying on his starboard hand.

Swiftly he made up his mind. He would take the angled shot at the right-hand *Littorio*, whose vast quarterdeck he could now see. She was in fact moored with her bows pointing towards the land and her stern to the harbour. All the better, thought Wellham. If he was lucky he would be able to blast her propellers and rudder to scrap iron.

Thirty feet above the surface of the water he levelled off and flew straight towards the enemy battleship. At five hundred yards range he pressed the grip and Humphreys, craning from the rear cockpit, saw the torpedo start to run.

Before the observer could draw in his head he was almost wrenched bodily out of his Sutton harness; the harbour and its madly firing ships spun dizzily before his eyes.

Wellham, feeling that slight jerk which told the pilot that his torpedo had gone, had in the same instant flung E.5H round in a tight turn that almost stood her on her wingtips. Then he sent the Stringbag roaring back eastward over the full width of the Mar Grande.

For a few fleeting seconds the Italian sailors in the cruisers and battleships had their elusive foe in their gunsights, and they hurled a tornado of shells and bullets in the wake of the fleeing plane.

'Intense anti-aircraft fire was directed towards the aircraft during the getaway,' stated Wellham's report primly.

E.5H did not escape without further damage. A 40-mm. shell exploded on the port wing, ripping a great gash in the fabric and shattering some of the wing ribs.

But that was the only hit scored by the enemy gunners as the Stringbag ran her lethal gauntlet, and she skimmed safely over the northern shore of San Pietro Island and raced away down the Gulf for home.

Despite flapping fabric and a bullet-holed fuselage. Wellham made such good time on the return journey to the carrier that he actually landed-on only three minutes after Hale, the leader.

Fifty miles astern of the second strike as they flew towards Taranto, a solitary Stringbag winged across the night sky, heading in the same direction. Swordfish L.5F was on her way at last, and Going was happy.

A big jovial man, George Robert Marshal Going son of a seaside medical practitioner, had entered the navy straight from school in 1931. Four years later he joined his first ship as an Acting Sub-Lieutenant, having gained two months' seniority as the result of obtaining a first-class pass in seamanship.

Fellow Sub-Lieutenants with him in that same year were Maund and Janvrin. Another ex-Dartmouth colleague was a tall, dark-haired youngster named Kerans, destined to earn post-war fame and a DSO by snatching the crippled frigate *Amethyst* from under the muzzles of Communist guns on the Yangtse river.

Going spent his early naval service in submarines. Then, in

1937, he decided to try his luck in a totally different element, the air. He volunteered for an observer's course in the Fleet Air Arm. With him on this venture went Alfie Sutton, and later when both had duly qualified for their observer's wings, they joined the carrier *Glorious* in the Mediterranean.

It was then that Going met Lyster for the first time, and he conceived a great admiration for the man whose tremendous faith in the bright future of naval aviation imbued the aircrews of his squadrons with a sense of destiny. Now Going and those who had served with him in those pre-war years were on their way to make Fleet Air Arm history.

When they took their lone departure from the *Illustrious* both Clifford and Going knew perfectly well that in their slow-flying plane they hadn't a hope of catching up with the rest of the squadron. But they were indifferent to the risks. They would swoop down to make their own attack just as the enemy was relaxing his guard, convinced that the night's raid was over. It was a situation they both relished.

Clifford took L.5F up to a cruising height of eight thousand feet, and at a speed of ninety knots they settled down to the 170-mile flight.

The journey was completely uneventful. But by 11.15 p.m., when they still had some fifty miles to go, they sighted that sinister glare in the heavens above Taranto. As the distance lessened the glow resolved itself into a ceaseless aurora of bursting shells.

'It was the biggest firework display we had ever seen,' said Going, 'and we were awestruck by it.'

While Hale and his torpedo-bombers were pressing home their attacks amid the earth-shaking din of the enemy barrage, L.5F continued to make her steady approach. Then as the last of the raiders fled from the harbour and climbed away over the Gulf, the gunfire faltered and died.

The lone Swordfish made her landfall five miles east of Taranto, and headed north-west over the town and dockyard to the far side of the Mar Piccolo. Gazing down from his cockpit, Going saw spread out below him the scene he had come to know so well from his study of those dog-eared reconnaissance photographs in the AIO of the *Illustrious*.

But now the waters of the harbour were streaked with huge patches which gave off a faintly luminous sheen; probably oil fuel, thought the airmen. Here and there ships were burning, and flames were shooting up from one of the battleships. The great attack seemed to have gone well.

Unhurriedly Clifford circled above the Mar Piccolo to make sure of his approach. 'Everything remained quiet while we stooged about,' said Going. 'The enemy must have thought we were a damaged aircraft limping around - or else they were deaf!'

Below them the airmen could see two enemy cruisers lying in mid-stream in the centre of the inner harbour, and close by them four anchored destroyers. Secured stern on to the dock-yard jetties lay four more cruisers, and on either side of them nearly a score of destroyers. From above in the moonlight the enemy vessels looked like fish nosing at the side of a pool.

Circling over the western mainland, Clifford brought L.5F down to 2,500 feet. Then he turned to port and dived almost vertically across the line of enemy ships. Peering over his head from the seat behind Going stared straight down at a big *Trento*-class cruiser that seemed to be racing up at him on an invisible lift.

At that moment the Italians opened fire. But with the Sword-fish, whistling into their midst at something like 150 miles an hour, her blue-green camouflage blending with the night sky, the gunners could only fire blindly.

At five hundred feet Clifford pulled out of the dive and let go his bombs. The whole stick of six appeared to drop squarely across two of the cruisers. But to the disgust of both airmen there were no resulting explosions.

Although they did not then know it, due to the thin plating of the Italian ships the British semi-armour-piercing bombs passed right through without exploding.

'The bloody things haven't gone off,' shouted Going. 'Shall we go round and try again?'

L.5F was now racing away down the southern bank of the Mar Piccolo, her route punctuated by streams of pom-pom shells from the enemy shore batteries.

'My dear Grubby,' came Clifford's acid retort over the Gos-port, 'I haven't the slightest intention of going through that lot again. We're off home.'

Still keeping low, he banked to port just short of the seaplane base Sarra had plastered so effectively earlier on, and skimmed across the water to the northern shore of the inner harbour. Then he swung L.5F sharply to starboard and with throttle wide sped away towards the sea.

Going turned to snatch a final glimpse of Taranto.

9 129

The glow of gunfire had died down. Columns of smoke writhed and weaved above the Mar Grande, and flames flickered redly in the battleship anchorage. With a weary but satisfied grin he settled back in his seat, reached for the chartboard and began to plot the return course. He had had a very tiring day.

CHAPTER X
THE RETURN

On board the *Illustrious* Captain Boyd awaited the return of the raiders with a feeling of intense anguish. Since the ship's arrival in the Mediterranean his airmen had carried out many offensive operations, for they considered it their duty to annoy the enemy as much as they could whenever possible.

The Italian bases of Rhodes and Leros in the Dodecanese had become familiar targets to them. But these enemy nests were strongly defended, and always before they set out to raid them Boyd warned the pilots not to stick their necks out.

'Drop your bombs from a fairly high level,' he told them, 'and take no unnecessary risks.'

But Taranto was different. This was a vital operation upon which perhaps the whole course of the war in the Mediterranean depended. This time he had told the aircrews that the did not want to see them back until the Italian fleet had been sunk.

Although the words had been spoken with mock ferocity he realised what such a dictum might mean. The pilots would regard it as an order and strain every nerve to carry it out, no matter what the hazards.

Many of them were bound to be knocked out. He would be damned lucky, he thought, to see even half of them come back.

Heedless of the fact that he himself had had no sleep for the past twenty-four hours, Boyd prowled restlessly about the compass platform, an unlighted pipe clenched between his teeth.

Admiral Lyster, too, was a prey to inner conflict as he kept a lonely vigil in his sea cabin. Aware of what was in the mind of his Commander-in-Chief, he knew that the attack on Taranto was a blow that had to be struck in the naval campaign against Italy.

For Lyster himself the venture was far more than the realisation of a desire to take revenge upon an enemy he despised; the success of the operation would provide resounding justification of his faith and that of others in the future destiny of the naval air arm.

He knew that the aircrews were confident of their ability to knock out the Italian fleet, preferring to ignore the possibility that they might have to pay a heavy price in casualties. In the cold-blooded balance sheet of war the loss of a handful of lives must be reckoned a very fair exchange for the destruction or crippling of an enemy fleet.

Nevertheless, as the slow minutes ticked past Lyster prayed fervently to the god of battles that the men who had finally set forth on this long-cherished mission might all be permitted to return safely.

In his cabin below decks Streamline Robertson had turned in fully dressed on his bunk. But he slept only fitfully, heaving himself up whenever he awoke to peer at the watch on his wrist. He was anxious, but philosophical. He had decided to go to bed soon after Morford and Green had landed-on their crippled L.5Q, for he knew that the first of the raiders to reach the target area could not be expected back until well after midnight. There was no sense in wasting energy.

No sense in worrying, either. He expected to miss some familiar faces when the squadron returned – *if* they returned, he had to prevent himself from adding. But the majority would be back, he was sure. They had been given all the training that was possible, and from their study of those excellent RAF photographs they knew perfectly well what was in store for them at Taranto.

There would be plenty to do when they returned. Some of the aircraft were bound to be shot up, and there might even be casualties at the last fence when they were landing-on. It would not do to lose any more: they were down to less than two squadrons as it was. Streamline dozed uneasily.

Except for the throbbing beat of her engines, the incessant hum of ventilation fans and the soft hiss of the water flowing past her speeding hull, the carrier herself seemed strangely quiet.

Guns' crews, closed up at their defence stations, lolled silently beside their weapons, some of the men dozing, others gazing vacantly out over the moonlit sea. The duty officers on the bridge spoke seldom, except to give a necessary order. Ratings catfooted about their duties as if fearing that the sound of their shipboard movements might be wafted over the sea to alert the Italians to an awareness of the danger speeding towards them through the skies. The accidental clatter of a boot on the rungs of a steel ladder jarred the nerves.

In the hangar below, which a few hours earlier had been the scene of frenzied activity, some of the lights had been switched off, and the folded wings of the Fulmar fighters, undercarriages and tail units securely fastened down to ring-bolts in the steel deck, cast deep pools of shadow. Huddled on benches or the top of tool boxes in odd corners of the hangar and engine workshops, fitters and riggers off watch sought uneasy sleep beneath spread greatcoats.

In the wardroom and officers' galley the stewards and cooks were busy. There were not only the next day's meals to be prepared. A special celebration was to be laid on for the returning aircrews. In addition to the bacon and eggs with which they would be regaled, Commander Tuck, the wardroom mess president, had ordered that the bar should be specially reopened for the airmen.

In his office the chief steward was laboriously printing a notice he intended to pin up in a prominent position in the mess. 'Welcome Back!' it announced in large red letters.

The chief cook's *pièce de résistance* graced the centre of the laid table. It was an outsize cake with a representation in the middle of a Swordfish aircraft fashioned out of pink icing sugar.

At seventeen knots the *Illustrious* and her escorts moved across the moonlit sea like a cluster of huge grey shadows. As soon as Clifford and Going had taken off in Swordfish L.5F, the carrier had reduced speed and turned to join the squadron on a course south-east by south. Distant to port the rugged coastline of the island of Cephalonia fringed the lip of the sea.

After steaming for some ninety minutes on this course, periodically zigzagging to fox any lurking enemy submarine, the carrier and her escorts would swing round in a 180-degree turn and head back in the opposite direction so as to approach position 'Y for Yorker', at about one o'clock in the morning. The *Illustrious* would then turn into wind and increase speed so as to work up a twenty-five-knot lift over the flight deck in readiness for the returning Swordfish to land-on.

But during the entire waiting period there could be no contact with the raiders. Wireless silence must remain absolute, to be broken only for a two-word signal from the strike leaders, 'Attack completed.'

Hunched now in his seat on the bridge, Boyd worried over the problem of recovering the aircraft. Many of them might be damaged and possibly unable to home on the carrier's beacon.

But if they could only make it as far as Cephalonia they might have a sporting chance of finding the cruising carrier.

Slowly the time passed while the squadron steamed along the south-easterly leg of the run. Nearly a hundred miles farther to the southward Cunningham with his battleships cruised watchfully.

The run was uneventful, and at eleven-thirty Lyster came out on to the flag bridge of the *Illustrious* as the carrier and her escorts swung ponderously round to take up the reciprocal course he had ordered earlier.

At one o'clock precisely, position 'Y for Yorker' was reached, and the ships closed in to within twenty miles of Cephalonia. Closely followed by her two attendant destroyers the *Illustrious* nosed into the wind and increased speed to twenty-one knots.

The first news of the returning planes would come from Schierbeck, the radar officer. Roused from his bunk soon after midnight, the eagle-eyed Canadian squatted in front of his precious set in the radar office and, with a tin of cigarettes at his side, settled down to a prolonged vigil.

At twelve minutes past one Schierbeck stiffened like a pointer and peered keenly at a blip which had appeared on the radar screen, to be followed soon afterward by another and another. He stubbed out his cigarette and turned to the seaman who stood at his elbow.

'That's them all right,' he grinned. 'Get on the blower and tell the bridge.'

As soon as he received the message from the radar office, Boyd put his night glasses to his eyes and scanned the heavens to the westward. Almost in the same instant the compass platform and the ship herself seemed suddenly to come to life. Air lookouts strained their gaze skywards; guns' crews scrambled to their feet and stared hopefully upwards. The slumbering fitters and riggers in the hangar and engine shop came awake and hurried up to the flight deck.

Warned by telephone, Robertson leapt from his bunk, grabbed his cap and swiftly climbed to the flying control platform. Peter Gregory, the Air Gunnery Officer, was already marshalling the flight deck personnel. The fire and crash parties were assembling with their gear. 'Haggis' Russell who, in the important role of batsman, would himself guide the returning Stringbags in, appeared from below carrying a pair of illuminated bats and an additional light hanging on his chest.

On the flag deck the Yeoman of Signals cradled an Aldis lamp in his arms, ready to acknowledge the aircrafts' recognition signals as they circled overhead.

Sparke and Neale in L.4C were the first to sight the carrier and her destroyer escort The spreading white wake of the *Illustrious* stood out like a pale ruler against the cloud-darkened surface of the sea. While Neale flashed their recognition signal, Sparke orbitted the carrier in the customary break-up circuit and, to lessen the risk of fire in case of crash landing, released the solitary flare which each of the torpedo droppers had carried.

Following them in to the circuit came Kiggell and Janvrin in L.4P. Macauley and Wray were the next to arrive, winking their recognition lights joyfully. Maund in E.4F, Lamb and Grieve in L.5B, Sarra and Bowker in L.4L, Forde and Mardel-Ferreira in L.4H, and Murray and Paine in E.5Q joined up in quick succession, sailing light-heartedly about the night sky as they shed their unused flares.

Below the circling Stringbags the carrier's flight deck was suddenly brilliantly outlined as deck and pillar lights were switched on to mark the line of approach.

Promptly L.4C as the first arrival turned into the down-wind leg and banked round for the land-on. With hawk-sharp eyes Sparke watched each flashing movement of Russell's lighted bats. But his approach was impeccable and, as he pointed the Stringbag at the carrier's round-down, he saw that the bat-man's arms were fully extended from his shoulders in the 'O.K.' signal.

With a sigh of relief Sparke pulled back the throttle, and a moment later felt the wheels brush the flight deck. They bounced once, then came the jerk of the arrester wire and they were down.

Dimly he was aware of rubber-capped figures rushing out to clear L.4C's tail hook. Ahead of him the crash barrier collapsed, and the Stringbag rolled forward to be instantly surrounded by the handling party, grinning and waving an excited welcome.

Astern the rest of the Swordfish were coming in at thirty-second intervals with the near precision of a normal daytime manoeuvre. Craning precariously out from the flying control platform, Robertson eagerly counted the Stringbags. Three . . . four . . . five. Some of the landings were bumpy, but men and planes looked to be in remarkably good shape.

Almost half the first strike were down now. The reports from Schierbeck indicated that he had eleven aircraft on the screen,

It seemed then that only one of the raiders had been unlucky; but it was too early to decide that yet.

At thirty-five minutes past one Patch and Goodwin in E.5A sighted the carrier and flashed their recognition signal. But there was no answering flash from below. They cruised around in silence as the minutes passed.

'What's up with the silly bastards?' snarled Ollie over the Gosport to Goodwin at last. 'They seem to be having a bloody fine party down there and no one's bothering about us.'

Bull in E.4F had picked up the carrier's beacon with thankfulness, since for ten minutes their Stringbag had been flying blind through cloud at four thousand feet. Soon he and Maund saw lights in the sky as more unused flares were released by their orbiting comrades, but below them there was still no sign of the *Illustrious*. Then at last Maund picked out the white wake of a destroyer and headed the Stringbag towards her.

In rapid succession Kemp in L.4K, Lamb in L.5B and Maund in E.4F landed-on. Once his tail hook had been released from the arrester wire, Kemp, in his excitement, moved off too fast and smashed into the tail of the taxying aircraft in front of him.

Robertson saw the crash and winced. In a sudden flash of anger he was about to despatch a messenger to summon the offending pilot before him, when he checked himself and grinned wryly.

'Hell,' he thought, 'you've done damned well tonight, my lad. I haven't the heart to give you a rocket after all you must have been through.'

Swayne and Buscall in L.4M sighted the carrier at 1.40 a.m., and ten minutes later turned out of the downwind leg and landed-on without difficulty.

Last of the first strike, Patch and Goodwin in E.5A, whose lights, unknown to them, had in fact failed, finally received the signal to land, and came in at five minutes to two. 'About time,' Ollie grumbled as he taxied forward.

That made eleven all safely recovered. The number exceeded everyone's wildest dreams. It was far, far better than Lyster, Boyd, or even Robertson, had dared to hope.

But who was missing?

As the identification letters and numbers of the returning aircraft were passed up to Robertson in flying control, the realisation sank in. The solitary casualty was Williamson, the strike leader. Had he bought it, then? Or was he just badly shot up and even now struggling to keep his crippled Stringbag in the air long enough to reach the vicinity of the waiting carrier?

The lookouts on the bridge turned their glasses skywards again. In the radar office Lieutenant Schierbeck glared fiercely at the blank face of the radar screen as if by sheer willpower he would force that last blip to appear.

Beyond the crash barrier the flight deck handling party worked swiftly and efficiently. As each Swordfish taxied up to them, the pilot cut his engine and folded the wings. The plane handlers wheeled the Stringbag on to the waiting lift and chocked the undercarriage. As the lift sank rapidly below, pilot and observer climbed stiffly out of their cockpits.

Stripping off their flying kit as they went, the aircrews struggled through the welcoming crowd in the hangar and up to the Air Intelligence Office for de-briefing.

Inside that small and crowded compartment lights glared, the atmosphere was thick with cigarette smoke, and a babel of excited voices filled the air. Everybody seemed to be talking at once, and Beale, seated at the table with a pile of report forms before him, was doing his best to extract a coherent narrative from pilots and observers as they thrust their way inside.

'Hell of a lot of flak, sir.'

'Yes, the blighters must have slung everything at us except the kitchen sink!'

'I didn't see any of those balloons, did you?'

'We did,' exclaimed Tony Wray proudly. 'Mac here went through the damned things twice!'

'So did I, and dropped my fish bang on, sir,' declared Sparke.

'How come we never saw the torpedoes explode?' demanded Kemp. 'We couldn't mistake the battle-wagons – even amongst all that hou-ha – and I'm sure I got a good run in at a *Littorio*.'

'That was because of the Duplex pistols,' explained Beale. 'You wouldn't be able to see much, I'm afraid.'

'I had a go at a *Littorio*, too,' said Maund. 'Had a good clear run in of a thousand yards. Yes, a good drop,' he confirmed in reply to Beale's query about torpedo release.

'What height did you have, then?' asked the Operations Officer.

'About thirty feet, I should think, sir.'

So the interrogation proceeded, and from these first impressions Beale, and Robertson, too, who had hurried down from flying control, knew that the attack had gone well.

But Swordfish L.4A was missing.

'Did anyone see what happened to Williamson?' shouted Beale presently.

Abruptly the babel of talk ceased, and each man glanced quickly at his neighbour. Then a voice spoke up. It was Sparke.

'I last saw him at four thousand feet over San Pietro island,' he said slowly. 'But that's all. Afraid I was too busy after that, sir.'

Beale shot a look at Streamline, who pursed his lips and gave a slight shrug. 'Doesn't sound too good,' he muttered, then turned and clove a way through them to the door.

'Must get back up top. The second strike is due in.'

The door closed behind him.

At five minutes to 2 a.m., Hale in L.5A and Skelton in L.4F sighted the steaming carrier below them. On the way back from Taranto the two pilots had spotted each other in the moonlight, and Skelton joined up with his leader.

They landed-on within seconds of one another, to be followed three minutes later by Wellham in E.5H, the bullet-torn fabric of his port wing flapping grotesquely.

At two-fifteen Torrens-Spence and Sutton in L.5K came in safely. They had had an easy trip back, marred only by gnawing anxiety as to the degree of damage their Stringbag might have suffered during those last hectic few minutes of the getaway.

At two-thirty Hamilton and Weekes in L.5B landed-on without incident, closely followed by Lea and Jones in L.5H. To his surprise Lea discovered that his undercarriage was still in place after all and seemingly undamaged.

The jettisoned flares of their team mates sailing about the sky had given them a scare, for the sight decided them that enemy fighters were about. Prudently Lea took L.5H down to sea level, and pilot and observer were greatly relieved when the *Illustrious* loomed up ahead of them.

Less than twenty minutes later Swordfish L.5F turned into the downwind leg above the carrier, and at two-fifty was duly batted in. Going's grinning face and waving arms acknowledged the enthusiastic cheers of the flight deck watchers.

The second strike had returned safely. And again only one aircraft was missing.

'This is fantastic!' muttered Robertson to 'Haggis' Russell as Clifford and Going vanished triumphantly below on the lift. 'Only two absentees out of twenty. Who's missing this time?'

'Bayly and Slaughter in E.4H,' the Flight Deck Officer told him. 'What an achievement, though, sir!'

'You're telling me,' grinned Streamline as he hurried off to the Air Intelligence office again.

Hale was making his report to Beale as Robertson pushed his way through the excitedly chattering aircrews.

'Dropped the fish about seven hundred yards from a *Littorio*,' the burly leader of the second strike was saying as the Commander (Flying) joined him.

'You must be feeling damned pleased with yourselves,' Streamline told him half enviously as Hale presently moved away and another pilot began to retail his story to the Operations Officer.

Then someone mentioned seeing an aircraft burning, and others added confirmation. Torrens-Spence and Sutton now came forward.

'That could have been the chap who was weaving about in front of us during our run in,' said the tall pilot of L.5K.

'I'm sure he got hit,' chimed in Alfie Sutton. 'I saw a flash as we got under him.'

'Well, that must have been Bayly and Slaughter, then. They're the ones who are missing,' announced Beale briefly before resuming his interrogation.

Maund heard that flat statement without surprise. He had talked to Bayly a few hours earlier while together they watched their Stringbags being armed. Gerry was always more jittery than most before a raid, but on this occasion his nervous state had been the worst Maund had ever found him in. As if he was possessed by a sort of horror, was how he expressed it to himself. Poor old Gerry!

From the AIO the aircrews filed up to the bridge to report their safe arrival to Boyd. Hale was the first to step forward and salute the dimly seen figure of his captain.

'5A returned, sir, please,' he stated formally.

'Glad to see you, Ginge. How did it go?' asked the smiling Boyd.

'Oh, all right, sir.'

'Did you get in a successful attack?'

'I think it might have been, sir.'

'Was there much flak?' Hell, do I have to tear it out of him, wondered Boyd.

'Quite a bit, sir. Any orders for the morning?'

A master of understatement, the imperturbable Hale. He seemed, said Boyd afterwards, completely indifferent to the whole show.

The squadron commander then reported to Lyster, who told him that the operation might have to be repeated that night, but that another senior pilot would lead the new strike. Hale then went down to his cabin and tore up the letter he had written to his wife in case he did not return. To this day she does not know what he had written.

The rest of the aircrews were almost as maddeningly laconic as Hale had been.

'Very glad to see you back,' said Boyd to Torrens-Spence and Sutton. 'What did you do?'

'Fired at a *Littorio*-class battleship, sir.'

'Did you hit her?'

'Can't say, sir. But we think the torpedo ran all right.'

Then it was Sparke's turn.

'Welcome home, Sparke. What did you do?'

'Went in through the balloons, sir. I reckoned I would not be fired at that way, and I was not.'

'And how did you come out?'

'I came back through the same hole, sir.'

Boyd asked Lea about the anti-aircraft fire.

'Was there anything personal?' he queried.

'The only thing was when I flew over the fore turret of a cruiser and she opened up at me,' replied the pilot in a matter-of-fact manner.

Boyd twitched a slightly sceptical eyebrow, but when later he inspected Swordfish L.5H he marvelled that the Stringbag had managed to return at all.

His abiding impression was of the astounding modesty of the aircrews. They had just returned from an operation of un-paralleled hazard, yet despite their excitement and elation at the successful accomplishment of their mission, they spoke of their experiences only in the most clipped and prosaic manner. Clearly they thought that what they had done was neither funny nor interesting. He wondered what the press boys would make of them when the *Illustrious* returned to Alexandria.

From the bridge the tired crews stumbled down to the ward-room. Here in the familiarity of warm, brightly lit surroundings the smiling stewards waited to welcome them.

Everyone crowded round the bar, and no one thought it odd to be drinking whisky and soda at well after three o'clock in the morning. It seemed as though days had passed instead of hours since they last stood in this same wardroom listening to Beale telling them of what lay ahead. Since then they had passed through a tremendous experience and an aeon of time. The chief steward's 'Welcome back' notice added to the latter impression.

Presently they sat down at the laid tables and found themselves devouring bacon and eggs with the ravenousness of men who had not eaten for days; and tired, overwhelmingly tired; chewed to a rag.

Then all at once the food became tasteless, and their elation left them. It suddenly became an effort to recall exactly what had happened during those brief yet ageless minutes in the target area; moments of fierce concentration; of near terror; and of unutterable relief to find themselves alive and still flying; the uncertainty of reaching the carrier on the return journey; the final safe landing.

Reaction was setting in, and here and there heads began to nod over half-emptied plates. The excitement flickered out like a snuffed candle, and the wardroom began to clear as one by one the exhausted airmen staggered to their feet and departed to seek the oblivion of sleep.

Some of the aircrews had been sleeping in camp beds on the quarterdeck, and ratings whose duties took them there tiptoed round the slumbering men. But the latter's rest was of short duration, for soon after dawn the 'Judgment' Force rejoined the fleet. Hale himself went round unceremoniously rousing the aircrews.

'Come on, you dozy bloody lot,' he exhorted them. 'Pull yourselves together. You've probably got to do the whole thing over again tonight.'

'Good God,' groaned one of the dog-tired pilots, 'they only asked the Light Brigade to do it once!'

As the *Illustrious* and her consorts came in sight of Cunningham's battleship squadron a string of bunting climbed slowly to the signal yard of the flagship, and streamed out in the wind.

On the flag deck of the carrier a grinning signalman jotted down the message on his pad. It was brief, to the point, and a classic understatement. But it was traditional and typical. The message read simply, '*Illustrious* manoeuvre well executed.'

Stilted? Niggardly praise? Not to the initiated, who knew that in the navy such a signal by a Commander-in-Chief to one of his ships is very rarely made.

Soon afterwards Admiral Cunningham sent another signal. This time it was addressed to 'General,' which meant that it was received by all ships and naval establishments in the British

Mediterranean Command. The message was the result of Beale's interrogation of the Swordfish crews a few hours earlier, and it read as follows: '*Illustrious* aircraft carried out most successful raid on Taranto. Estimated that one *Littoro* and two *Cavour* torpedoed and many fires started by bombs. All aircraft returned except two.'

The fleet was jubilant, but confirmation of the airmen's success was eagerly awaited. There were two sources from which this would come: the enemy himself, and from Squadron Leader Whiteley and his faithful band in 431 Flight at Malta.

As the day wore on and the British ships swept in majestic formation back and forth across the Ionian Sea between Greece and Sicily, an official Italian radio communique was snatched from the ether by the warship's listening wireless staffs.

'In the early hours of last night,' announced the broadcaster in Rome, 'enemy aircraft attacked the naval base at Taranto. The anti-aircraft defences of the base and of the ships anchored there reacted violently. Only one unit was in any way extensively damaged. There are no victims. Six enemy aircraft were shot down and part of their crews captured. Three others were also probably shot down.'

This announcement caused almost as much sardonic amusement in the *Illustrious* as an earlier enemy radio statement someone had monitored, which declared that 'desperadoes' had attacked Taranto and that hundreds of them had been shot down.

But all agreed that if the Italians had been forced to admit that one unit was badly damaged, then the claim that heavy casualties had been inflicted on the raiders was an attempt to belittle the severity of the attack. And the statement that some of the aircrews had been captured gave reason for hope that Williamson and Scarlett, Bayly and Slaughter might have survived after all.

However, more reliable news was on the way. For at first light on November 12th, Whiteley himself had taken off from Malta to have, as he expressed it, 'a looksee at Taranto'.

But first he had to carry out a patrol from Malta to Corfu. For in the early hours of that morning the British Ambassador in Ankara had signalled to the Commander-in-Chief that he had received news of an intended attack by the Italian fleet on Corfu.

His reconnaissance along the scheduled patrol line duly completed without result, Whiteley finally arrived above Taranto

What he saw below gave him, in his own words, 'more lift than a case of Scotch.'

So far as his trained eye could tell, one of the Italian battleships was in the process of being beached. Huge patches of fuel oil surrounded those that were still at their moorings, in the Mar Grande. Other ships were being shifted to new berths.

But Whiteley was not permitted to remain for long in the area. The defenders were still very touchy, and soon the sky around him was heavily pockmarked with the black and brown smoke of shellbursts. Making a second run over the harbour, Whiteley suddenly spotted an Italian fighter coming at him head on.

Fortunately the enemy plane was slightly higher and moving too fast to fire its guns at the moment of encounter. As the fighter whistled overhead Whiteley opened his throttle wide and fled from the scene as hard as he could go.

When he was clear of danger the squadron leader despatched a brief coded reconnaissance report to Malta, adding in a restrained postscript, 'One enemy battleship sinking.' He was sorely tempted to embellish the message and compliment the navy upon its undoubted success, but decided to wait until he landed back at Luca when his crews' impressions could be added to the general picture.

Whiteley's morsel of information was duly passed on to the waiting fleet with the warning that some hours would have to elapse before the photographs he had taken could be processed and interpreted, and a full official appreciation made of them.

In the meantime the Italians attempted to hit back at their foes. They sent out reconnaissance planes to try to locate the British warships. Squadrons of bombers waited on Italian airfields to launch massive attacks the moment Cunningham's fleet was pinpointed.

But now it was the turn of the fighters from the *Illustrious* to go into action. Two of the questing enemy seaplanes were picked up on the carrier's radar while yet some miles distant, pounced on by her Fulmars and ignominiously shot down. A third enemy machine got close enough to spot the fleet and then fled for the shelter of cloud cover. But, outpaced and outmanoeuvred by pursuing British fighters, the lumbering Cant was sent spinning out of the sky before the Italian airmen could get off their all-important sighting report.

In the carrier's hangar below decks fitters and riggers were working all out to prepare the scarred and oil streaked Swordfish for the planned repeat attack on Taranto that night.

For this second operation fifteen aircraft would form the striking force; six to carry torpedoes, seven to act as dive-bombers and two to carry flares. As next senior pilot to Hale now that Williamson had gone, Patch had been detailed to lead the force. Choice of crews was being left until the last moment.

Admiral Cunningham had agreed to this second attack being made in response to Lyster's urging. Less than half an hour after Clifford and Going had landed-on, the Rear-Admiral, impressed by the unanimous plea of the aircrews to finish the job, had drafted the following message to the Commander-in-Chief, which was sent by visual signal to the flagship when the Judgment Force rejoined Cunningham.

'Although the AA fire was very heavy, aircraft crews feel that now they know the way they would like to repeat the attack as soon as possible. In view of the inevitable strengthening of the defences which may frustrate attempts at a later date, I do most earnestly urge that Judgment be repeated tonight if possible.'

The new attack was to be made subject to continued reconnaissance being possible, the weather remaining suitable, and provided that the fleet could succeed in eluding enemy observation throughout the day.

But two Fleet Air Arm bites at the cherry, Cunningham decided, would be enough. 'After tonight 12-13 November,' he signalled to the Air Officer Commanding, Mediterranean, 'Taranto is your bird.'

As the day wore on Boyd began to worry about the coming operation. He knew that the aircrews had had little or no sleep, and despite their cheerfulness they were showing signs of strain. The defenders of Taranto would be expecting them and their reception would be even hotter than before. Boyd was determined that there should be no sacrifice of lives. Furthermore, the weather was steadily deteriorating and banks of low cloud were obscuring the sky.

The Commander-in-Chief had evidently been thinking along the same lines, for at three minutes to four that afternoon he signalled to Lyster: 'I am relying on your judgement to give up the operation tonight if for any reason you feel it is not feasible or if it is asking too much of the Fleet Air Arm. I am as anxious as you and they are to put the finishing touch on last night's fine effort but don't allow this to bias your judgment.'

But by six o'clock that evening the weather had become too bad for flying, and the meteorological outlook for the next twelve hours gave no indication of any improvement being likely. Accordingly Admiral Cunningham cancelled the operation, and the fleet shaped course for Alexandria.

Two and a half hours later came the first definite news of the results of Operation Judgment. It was a signal from the Vice-Admiral Commanding at Malta.

'While I do not wish unduly to raise hopes,' began the message cautiously, 'it definitely appears as a result of examination of the reconnaissance photographs that (a) one *Littorio*-class battleship is down by the bows with her forecastle awash and a heavy list to starboard. Numerous auxiliaries alongside; (b) one *Cavour*-class battleship beached opposite the entrance to the graving dock under construction. Stern including Y turret is under water. Ship is heavily listed to starboard; (c) inner harbour; two cruisers are listed to starboard and are surrounded by oil fuel; (d) two auxiliaries off commercial basin appear to have sterns under water. Hearty congratulations on great effort.'

This was magnificent. Coupled with the news that while Taranto was taking a pounding Admiral Pridham-Wippell with his light forces had fallen on and practically annihilated an Italian convoy in the Straits of Otranto made the night of November 12th on board the *Illustrious* one to be remembered.

At long last the Fleet Air Arm had put itself fairly and squarely on the map.

CHAPTER XI

BLACK DAY FOR ITALY

As midnight came and went on November 11th, 1940, and the moon outside highlighted the domes, arches and basilicas of Rome, a handful of high-ranking Italian naval officers stood grouped in the operations room of Supermarina gazing with horrified concentration at a growing picture of disaster.

For almost an hour news of dire happenings had been coming in from the naval base at Taranto where Campioni's fleet was being heavily attacked in its own defended harbour by enemy bombers and torpedo planes.

When the final decisive warning that raiders were approaching had been received over the direct landline from Taranto, Admiral Cavagnari himself had gone along to the operations room in Supermarina to see how the threat would be met and repulsed. Now he sat staring unbelievingly at a pile of message forms which lay before him. At his side was Somigli, monocle firmly in place, striving to preserve an outward calm in these moments of catastrophe. Other officers stood about with stricken faces, pale and silent. One captain furtively wiped tears from his eyes.

As the air attack developed in intensity casualty reports streamed in relentlessly.

'*Duilio* hit.'

'*Cavour* holed and taking water fast.'

'Two torpedo strikes on the *Littorio*.'

'A bomb has pierced the deck of the *Trento*.'

'The *Libeccio* has been hit.'

Three battleships, a large cruiser and a fleet destroyer all damaged, perhaps mortally, within the space of minutes!

A second attack followed almost on the heels of the first. The *Littorio* hit a third time. Fires raging in the seaplane station; in the dockyard; in the oil depot; ships straddled by bombs.

Then, more ominously, 'The *Cavour* is sinking, but the *Littorio* still afloat, the *Duilio* also.'

Supermarina was appalled. 'It was as if,' said one of the staff officers, 'we had lost a great naval battle and could not foresee being able to recover from the consequences.'

Meanwhile, down at Taranto consternation was equally pro-
found and confusion reigned. With the departure of the last
enemy aircraft an immense pall of smoke hung over the harbour
area. The atmosphere was heavy with the acrid reek of explosives.

Fires were still blazing in some of the damaged ships whose
officers and men fought to subdue the flames. Damage-control
teams strove to confine flooding to the fewest underwater compartments. Engineers stumbled about amid wreckage and
smouldering debris trying to ascertain the extent of the havoc.
Electricians worked by the glow of torches below decks to repair
shattered lighting and power circuits. Doctors tended the
wounds of the injured and administered morphia to the dying.

In the dockyard firefighting vessels, tugs and repair craft
were hastily being cast off to go to the aid of stricken vessels.
From Admiral Riccardi's headquarters ashore signal lamps
winked incessantly to each ship in turn. 'Do you need assistance?'
'Have you any casualties?'

On board the fleet flagship Campioni's staff officers began
hurriedly to compile a summary of events from which an overall
assessment of the results of the great assault could be made,
and the morning's claims of a triumphant enemy refuted or, at
least, minimized.

Observers' accounts established that two separate attacks by
torpedo aircraft had taken place, following the dropping of a
number of brilliant parachute flares to the eastward of the Mar
Grande. These had created an intense zone of light against
which the hulls of the battleships had been all too clearly outlined.

The torpedo planes had come in three at a time in V formation from the westward at a low altitude, and launched their
torpedoes at a height of no more than thirty feet above the water.
Bombs had been dropped simultaneously by other aircraft.

Signals received from individual ships of the fleet graphically
described the events of the next action-packed eighteen minutes.

From *Cavour*: 'Loud explosions heard under the hull between
the conning tower and the second turret.'

From *Littorio*: 'Hit by torpedo on starboard bow.' And a few
minutes later: 'Hit on port quarter.'

From *Doria*: 'Two bombs have fallen in the sea ahead of us.'

From *Duilio* : 'Explosion observed in sea near starboard
quarter of *Littorio*.'

From *Libeccio* : 'Hit by bomb which did not explode. Other
ships straddled by bombs.'

From *Cavour* : 'Aircraft which attacked us fell in sea near floating dock.'

Thus, although the Swordfish crews of the *Illustrious* were not to learn the full results of their raid until after Italy's surrender in 1943, three of the six torpedoes fired in Williamson's attack found their marks. The strike leader's own torpedo had run successfully and exploded beneath the *Cavour*. Those launched by Kemp and Swayne were responsible for the first two hits sustained by the *Littorio*. Sparke's and Macauley's torpedoes both missed the *Andrea Dorea* at which they had been aimed, but had exploded beyond her, denting the ship's hull. Her lookouts thought the explosions had been made by heavy bombs.

The blast near the stern of the *Littorio* which had been seen by observers in the *Duilio* was caused by the explosion of Maund's torpedo, which unfortunately hit a mud bank and blew up.

As the second attack developed more signals had come in to the flagship telling of fresh successes by the raiders.

From *Duilio*: 'Struck by torpedo on starboard side.'

From *Littorio* : 'Hit on the starboard side by torpedo.'

From *Trento* : 'Hit forward by bomb.'

When subsequently the British and Italian accounts of heavy raid were compared it was possible to establish that the torpedo which struck the *Duilio* was launched by Lea in L.5H. Two more torpedoes had been fired at the *Littorio* – by Hale and Torrens-Spence. Only one of those hit the target; the other dived into the muddy sea bed and failed to explode. But the presence of this touchy intruder caused considerable alarm until divers could be sent down to locate it and render it harmless.

The bomb hit on the *Trento* was scored by Swordfish L.5F which, had he known of it, would greatly have cheered 'Grubby' Going.

As the details were filled in and a preliminary report drawn up to be sent off to Supermarina, it became clear that the British attack had been no haphazard affair, but a unique and devastating form of aerial assault. And the full results were yet to be properly appreciated.

Tugs, rescue and salvage craft were busy throughout the rest of the night. The *Duilio* had taken a lot of water aboard, and at a quarter to five in the morning she was hauled inshore and beached with her bows resting on the mud. The *Cavour* was in even worse condition. Fifteen minutes after the *Duilio* had been beached she was towed into shallow water and her crew taken off in case she should founder. The stricken *Littorio*, which was listing by the bows and had her forepart awash, was also moved closer inshore as a precautionary measure.

When dawn came the twin harbours of Taranto presented a very different aspect from that of the day before. The surface of the Mar Grande was partially covered by a vast and slowly spreading film of oil. Close to the fuelling jetty in the southeast corner sprawled the crippled hulk of the *Conte di Cavour*. The battleship was heavily listed to starboard, and from her riven plates a thick stream of fuel oil ebbed away like the lifeblood of a dying monster. The whole of her stern and the starboard side of her upper deck were under water. At eight o'clock that morning her weakened bulkheads gave way and she settled down on the bottom.

Six hundred yards away from her lay the *Littorio*, her bows still partly awash. A flotilla of small craft was clustered round the damaged battleship, their crews working frantically to salvage the great vessel.

Alongside her port quarter a tanker was made fast, her pumps sucking back the precious oil fuel into her tanks to lighten the larger vessel and counter the weight of seawater which had flooded inboard. A naval auxiliary was secured to the starboard side to provide meals and temporary accommodation for the *Littorio's* crew, whose own messdecks and cabins were flooded. An ocean-going submarine nestled alongside the auxiliary, her batteries supplying the crippled giant with electric power in place of the latter's own dynamos, which had been put out of action. Half a dozen tugs nuzzled round the listing hulk with their towing wires ready for action at short notice.

In the northward arc of the anchorage the third damaged capital ship, the *Caio Duilio*, lay with her bows aground and salvage vessels, similarly engaged, alongside.

Inside the Mar Piccolo two *Trento*-class cruisers wallowed in a sea of their own oil fuel which was leaking from their damaged tanks. Boats scurried about from ship to ship. Ambulances waited on the jetties. Firemen and salvage parties were still at work amid the charred and smoking ruins of a hangar building in the seaplane base.

Along the waterfront anxious civilians had congregated to gaze out across the murky waters with glum and despondent faces. There had been few casualties in the town, but their pride was hurt. The crippling of the fleet was almost as great a blow to them as to the sailors themselves.

Later that morning Admiral Riccardi convened a conference of flag officers and ship's captains, the commandant of the port's defences and senior dockyard officials. From the mass of signals and reports which had been accumulating in his office he reconstructed the events of the night.

First the raid itself.

The leading flight of enemy aircraft had appeared over the San Vito area shortly before 11 p.m., and dropped flares with the object of silhouetting the battle squadron.

Barrage fire was therefore concentrated on the western approaches to the harbour following reports that aircraft were coming in from that direction. The first ship to go into action was the *Cavour*, who opened fire at five minutes past eleven with all her close-range weapons, following the prediction of her AA indicators. But no enemy plane was seen and she soon ceased fire.

Five minutes later the *Duilio* opened up, her machine guns joining in the furious barrage fire which was now directed at the zone between Cape San Vito and San Pietro island.

It was through this hail of shells and bullets that Williamson, Sparke and Macauley were making their run-in.

At fourteen minutes past eleven a lookout on board the *Cavour* spotted a torpedo plane heading towards the battleship, and her machine guns reopened fire. Almost at once the gunners were rewarded by the sight of the aircraft falling into the sea in an upthrown column of spray.

But an unpleasant surprise was speeding swiftly towards them. A few seconds later the ship whipped and shuddered under the impact of a violent explosion. The plane had already launched its torpedo before being shot down.

At the same time as the *Cavour* was hit the *Littorio* was struck almost simultaneously by two torpedoes, one on the starboard bow and the other on the port quarter. A split second later another explosion occurred near her starboard quarter which was seen and reported by the *Caio Duilio*. Although the battleship had been holed by the two torpedo hits and her plating was dented by the third explosion, a quick check-up convinced her captain that the damage was not severe.

While all this was going on in the Mar Grande the ships and batteries inside the inner harbour were directing intense fire at low-flying aircraft which were dropping bombs. Destroyers at the pens were straddled by bombs, one of which struck the *Libeccio* but fortunately did not explode. Another fell in the water just ahead of the destroyer *Lanciere*.

Scarcely had the sound of aircraft engines begun to fade after this daring assault than more flares blossomed above the Mar Grande. The fortress barrage was reopened at full strength and was joined soon afterwards by short-range weapons from some of the tankers anchored in the commercial basin. These ships reported that a flight of aircraft with their engines cut out was diving towards the cruisers *Zara* and *Gorizia*. Both vessels opened violent fire with their machine guns.

This was the welcome which greeted Hale and his men of the second striking force who were approaching the harbour over Cape Rondinella.

Within seconds of the new attack developing spotters in the *Duilio* reported that a torpedo plane was heading towards their ship at a very low altitude, and the battleship opened fire with her close-range weapons. The aircraft was seen to fire its torpedo at a range of about 450 yards, after which the machine turned away at a steep angle across the battleship's bows. It was pursued by rapid bursts of machine-gun fire and was believed to have been shot down.

Meanwhile the torpedo launched by the British pilot struck the *Duilio* on the starboard side of the ship, abreast of No. 2 turret and well below the waterline.

One minute later the *Littorio* sustained a third hit. Two aircraft had come in to attack the battleship, one of which had actually been seen by Campioni's deputy chief of staff in the *Vittorio Veneto*. He had noticed heavy flak going up over the merchant ship harbour and guessed from this that enemy planes were making for the battleship anchorage. The torpedo launched by the second of these aircraft did not appear to have exploded. Subsequently, as already related, it was found in the mud beneath the *Littorio's* keel.

One plane was claimed to have been shot down in this attack. This was in fact the luckless E.4H crewed by Bayly and Slaughter.

For fifty minutes, from shortly after midnight until one o'clock in the morning enemy aircraft made repeated bombing attacks upon warships in the Mar Piccolo. One stick of six fell without exploding. Four fell into the water between the cruiser *Trento* and a nearby destroyer; one landed on the *Trento* near the cruiser's bridge, and the sixth plunged into the sea between two other destroyers. More bombs were dropped on land near a factory.

Four high-explosive bombs and several incendiaries were dropped on the seaplane base. One of the bombs exploded inside a hangar and destroyed two aircraft which were being repaired

This bomb also started a fire which was not brought under control for fifteen minutes.

Six more bombs had fallen near the oil storage depot. All of them exploded, but the only damage caused was the fracturing of a supply pipe.

Dockyard officials reported that three bombs fell near one of the basins, causing slight damage. Incendiaries started a number of fires, but all of these were soon extinguished. Of eleven HE bombs which fell near a storehouse, four exploded resulting in minor damage only. Seven others were dropped close to some electrical workshops and a nearby aqueduct was damaged.

As regards the town itself, some of the British bombs had fallen near a civilian hospital, but they caused no casualties. Others, however, had wrecked a number of houses in the vicinity of the dockyard and injured some of the occupants.

Gunfire, said the fortress commander, had ceased at five minutes to 1 a.m., and at twenty-two minutes past that hour the 'all clear' was sounded. Their chief could scarcely admit the fact, but the fortress gunners had become so jittery that for a quarter of an hour after the last enemy aircraft had departed they had continued firing wildly in all directions at nothing!

Logistics of the battle showed that a total of 13,489 rounds had been blasted off by the shore AA defences. The 4-inch batteries had fired nearly 1,750 and the 3-inch guns close on 7,000 rounds. The remainder had been fired by the pom-pom guns and other automatic weapons.

Ships' fire had been confined to machine guns, but no details of the number of rounds the navy's gunners had got off were available at the conference. The fleet was far too busy on urgent salvage work to bother with statistics of ammunition expended.

Casualties inflicted on the enemy were claimed to be six air-craft. One of these had fallen into the sea near the floating dock. Another was seen burning outside the breakwater between San Pietro island and Cape Rondinella. A third was reported to have crashed in flames off San Vito, and a fourth near the Chiappero jetty. A fifth was shot down off San Paolo islet, and the sixth, seen to have been struck by bursts of machine-gun fire from the cruisers in the Mar Grande, dipped close to the water, then turned sharply away and vanished.

Now came details of the injuries suffered by the fleet.

Personnel losses were comparatively light. Twenty-three men had been killed in the *Littorio*, sixteen in the *Cavour* and one in the *Duilio*. But the material damage was grave indeed.

The hit on the starboard bow of the *Littorio* had torn a gaping wound in her hull between the bilge-pump station and the cable locker, measuring forty-nine feet by thirty-two feet. Hundreds of tons of water had poured through this gap and flooded the fore part of the ship.

The second torpedo hit on the same side had struck farther aft, the blast narrowly missing the foremost turret magazine. This rent measured forty by thirty feet in size, and No. 1 magazine had in fact been flooded by the invading sea.

The third torpedo had ripped open the plating along the battleship's port quarter for a distance of some twenty-five feet abreast the steering compartment. Water pouring in here had added seriously to the internal flooding. In addition the plating on the starboard quarter was badly dented by the explosion of the torpedo which had near-missed the ship. It was obvious that the *Littorio* would be out of action for months.

The torpedo which struck the *Duilio* had ripped a hole in her starboard side measuring more than eight hundred square feet in area. The subsequent inrush of water had completely flooded Nos. 1 and 2 magazines. She, too, would require extensive docking and repairs. Only by partially beaching the ship had it been possible to save her from foundering.

The *Cavour* was in worst case of all. The enemy torpedo had blasted an enormous wound in her side through which sea-water had flooded in and drowned the forward compartments entirely. Remaining bulkheads had given way under the terrific strain and she had now sunk. No estimate could be made of the repair possibilities until the ship was lifted from the sea bed and pumped dry

In fact, although the *Cavour* was afterwards successfully raised, repairs to the vessel had not been completed by the time the war ended.

The damage caused to ships by enemy bombs was not serious. The cruiser *Trento* had a hole punched through her main deck and blast damage to bulkheads and ventilating pipes. The port bow of the destroyer *Libeccio* had been fractured, and the shield and part of the training gear of the foremost gun smashed. The hull plates of the destroyer *Pessagno* were distorted below the waterline as the result of near-misses.

In the final review of events Riccardi declared that the attack had not come as a surprise since ships and shore defences had been alerted for more than two hours previously.

The net defences had not been fully in place. If they had

been it was possible that only the *Duilio* would have been hit. Yet the torpedo strikes were so low that it was obvious they had been set to run deep, and nets might well have been useless anyway. In addition the British had used a new and deadly type of pistol.

Only a small number of aircraft had been hit. Thus the defences had proved unsatisfactory in view of the enormous number of rounds fired. But their lack of success could be partly accounted for by the British airmen remaining at a high level until they dived down to make their individual attacks. They were thus able to keep above the barrage fire. The enemy torpedo planes only became visible when they had approached to within yards of their objectives. Ships' gunners in general fired only at vague noises.

Finally Riccardi generously admitted that the British attack had been carried out with expert skill and daring.

With this summing up Campioni agreed.

When Count Ciano, Mussolini's Foreign Minister, learned of the disaster he wrote in his diary: 'A black day. The British, without warning, have attacked the Italian fleet at anchor in Taranto and have sunk the dreadnought *Cavour* and seriously damaged the battleships *Littorio* and *Duilio*. These ships will remain out of the fight for many months. I thought I would find the Duce downhearted. Instead he took the blow quite well and does not at the moment seem to have fully realised its gravity. When Badoglio last came to see me at the Palazzo Chigi he said that when we attacked Greece we should immediately have to move the fleet, which would no longer be safe in the port of Taranto. Why was this not done a fortnight after the beginning of operations and with a full moon?'

In an earlier moment of frankness Mussolini had confessed his ignorance of naval matters. Like Hitler, he had no conception of the importance of sea power. He was now to reap the fruits of his neglect.

Nevertheless, heads had to roll. Cavagnari was relieved of his post as Chief of the Naval Staff and Admiral Riccardi took over in his place. Somigli also went, and Supermarina saw him no more. In the meantime the undamaged ships of the Italian battlefleet were hastily moved up to Naples.

When the news of this move reached the British Mediterranean Fleet, Boyd and his Swordfish crews grinned happily. After all, that had been one of the objects of the exercise.

CHAPTER XII

SWORDFISH L.4A

LIEUTENANT RUGGIERO STELLA of the Italian destroyer *Fulmine* had been on deck for nearly two hours when the fortress guns of Taranto opened their thunderous barrage.

The 1,220-ton *Fulmine*, belonging to the Eighth Destroyer Division, was moored at the most southerly point of the battleship anchorage in the Mar Grande. She lay with her bows pointing at the Tarantola mole and her stern towards the battleship *Conte di Cavour*, anchored some four hundred yards to the northward. Away on her port bow loomed the great ungainly bulk of the floating dock, and some three hundred yards to starboard lay the destroyer *Trelumi*.

The *Fulmine* was armed with four 4.7-inch guns in twin mountings, one pair sited on the forecastle and the other on the after bandstand. Amidships she carried six torpedo tubes in two triple mountings. Abaft her single stubby funnel was a circular steel platform upon which was mounted a small battery of close-range weapons. On the night of November 11th Lieutenant Stella was officer in charge of this secondary armament.

Little had happened since the guns' crews of the destroyer, along with those of the rest of the fleet, had been piped to action stations when the fortress alert had sounded at 9 p.m. The lieutenant and his steel-helmeted gunners had grown bored with the inaction; but now as they stood to their weapons their faces looked pale and scared in the ghastly radiance of the slowly descending British parachute flares.

As the heavy guns of the port's AA defences filled the air with the scream and crash of bursting shells, the sharper tearing sound of machine guns came from the battleship astern of the *Fulmine*, and jets of coloured tracer spurted past a few yards from the destroyer's starboard side. The *Cavour's* close-range weapons had opened fire at an unseen target. The *Fulmine's* gunners fingered their triggers and waited tensely. Presently the *Cavour* fell silent, but the gunfire of the shore defences redoubled in fury. Nervously Lieutenant Stella scanned the moonlit heavens in search of the enemy.

At fourteen minutes past eleven the *Cavour* opened fire again, the tracers from her machine guns soaring now over the mastheads of the *Fulmine* like coloured fountains.

Almost in the same instant Lieutenant Stella saw an aircraft winging towards his ship in the path of the moon. At once he recognised it as a torpedo plane. With engine cut out the machine was diving on to the *Fulmine* at high speed. It was not more than a thousand yards away.

He screamed an order to his men, and a .8-inch gun opened rapid fire at the enemy plane. The first stream of bullets went wide, but presently the gunner's aim steadied and the tracers began to converge on the diving aircraft. A .52-inch gun then opened up, and as its bullets, too, found the target, Stella's lips parted in an exultant grin.

Almost at once the enemy plane turned to starboard, the engine roaring as the pilot switched on full power. Gripping the rail in his excitement, Stella saw a torpedo leap from the belly of the aircraft and plunge into the sea. Clearly visible in the light of the moon and flares the bubbling torpedo track appeared. It was arrowing straight towards the *Cavour* astern.

But it was evident that the enemy machine had been hit. With its wings rocking wildly the plane skidded over the bows of the *Fulmine* and headed towards the floating dock as the pilot sought desperately to gain height. The yelling destroyer gunners swung their weapons round in pursuit, and under the hail of their machine-gun bullets the aircraft suddenly lurched in mid-flight. Then its nose dipped and the plane crashed into the harbour and sank rapidly.

When Williamson came to, for the *Fulmine*'s victim was indeed Swordfish L.4A, he found himself trapped in his seat beneath a suffocating weight of water. The last thing he remembered was a hosepipe of tracer lashing out at his Stringbag as he fled past an enemy destroyer.

His forehead throbbed painfully. He must have banged it against the instrument panel when they crashed. Abruptly full realisation of his predicament screamed into his mind.

'Oh God,' he thought, 'I'm going to be drowned!'

But the overpowering instinct of self-preservation drove his numbed body into frantic action. He struggled to unfasten his parachute, and to his surprise it fell off just as he had always been told it would. A cynic, he had never quite believed that the release gear would work properly in an emergency. He jabbed the button that released his Sutton harness, and that worked too.

With his lungs almost at bursting point and his head pounding and throbbing, Williamson kicked himself free of the cockpit and shot up to the surface.

As he floundered on to his back and sucked in great gulps of life-giving air, he became aware of another figure splashing about beside him. It must be Scarlett.

'You all right, Blood?' he gasped.

The observer spat water. 'Yes, I'm OK, Ken,' he said. 'I thought you'd had it, though.'

Still partially dazed by the blow on his head, Williamson stared foggily about him. A few yards away the tail fin of the sinking Swordfish was sticking up at a grotesque angle and raindrops seemed to be falling around it. Then the pilot came to with a jerk when he suddenly realised that the splashes were not caused by rain or falling shrapnel. Someone was firing a machine gun at them!

'Let's get to hell out of here,' he yelled to Scarlett, 'and try to make it to that floating dock.'

'My ruddy oath, chum,' agreed the observer fervently, and the two struck out for the dock as hard as they could.

They had a distance of about one hundred and fifty yards to cover, but to the sick and dizzy Williamson the journey seemed endless. Scarlett reached the dock first and guided his exhausted pilot to a ringbolt which hung down about a foot above them. Williamson clung on desperately, his chilled and soaking body rasped by the barnacled dock plating.

Flashes from the soaring gunfire illuminated their position, and darts of tracer criss-crossed a few feet above the surface of the water. The airmen decided that it was time to move on.

Just as Williamson released his grip on the ringbolt an accurately aimed burst of machine gun fire struck fiery sparks from the metal, and bullets whined and ricochetted all round them.

They swam a few yards farther along, then decided to climb into the dock itself. This feat they accomplished with difficulty. Scratched and bleeding, since they each wore only a shirt, shorts and a Mae West, they finally collapsed on the floor of the dock. Then came a sudden rush of footsteps and in a moment they were surrounded by a crowd of yelling Italians.

The airmen were pounced on and dragged to their feet by their captors, who turned out to be dockyard workmen; 'the scum of Naples, I should think,' commented Williamson afterwards. One ruffian, who appeared to be their foreman, drove a pistol into the pilot's ribs and swore ferociously at him.

His men, screaming and yelling, literally tore the scanty clothes from their captives' bodies. Then, naked and shivering, the airmen were hustled along to a hut on the dock. Inside the workmen crowded round them, shouting obscenities and insults and making threatening gestures. Neither Williamson nor Scarlett understood Italian, and expected to be lynched at any moment. However, after a while the Italians calmed down somewhat, and on the order of the foreman the airmen were thrown a blanket each with which to cover themselves.

Under the lowering gaze of their captors they waited, huddled and shivering while the bedlam of the raid continued. At last, after nearly an hour had dragged by, the guns fell silent. Suddenly the hut door was thrust open and the foreman entered, accompanied by two armed Italian sailors.

The airmen were seized and hustled out. Waiting alongside the dock was a naval motorboat. Prodded by the sailors, they clambered down into the boat, which immediately shoved off and headed towards a nearby destroyer. It was in fact the *Fulmine*.

Angry and humiliated to have been robbed of their clothes but thankful to have escaped with whole skins from the clutches of the dock crew, the airmen clutched their blankets tightly around them and gingerly climbed aboard the destroyer. As they padded over the gangway an Italian officer came forward and addressed Williamson.

'Sei ferito?' he asked, not unkindly.

But since the pilot had not the faintest idea that this query meant, 'Are you wounded?' he could do nothing but remain silent and shake his head uncomprehendingly.

The lieutenant shrugged, and led the way below. In the destroyer's warmly lit wardroom the captain and two other officers stood up to greet them. One of the latter, a lieutenant who spoke English fairly well, then seated himself at a table and began to interrogate the captured airmen. Mindful of the Geneva Convention they gave only their names and ranks.

'And what are your numbers?' asked the lieutenant, after carefully writing down their replies.

'We have no numbers,' said Williamson curtly.

'Niente numero!' exclaimed the captain in surprise when this was interpreted to him. 'Non lo credo. Ancora domandi a loro,' he commanded.

But Williamson insisted that the Royal Navy did not in fact follow the universal military practice of conferring an identity number upon its officers, and that therefore they were not concealing permissible information. The Italians were at last convinced, and the atmosphere immediately became very cordial. An officer who spoke French offered the captives a glass of brandy, and the captain himself went to rummage in his cabin for some spare clothing to give them.

Food and beer were then brought and placed before the Englishmen. So far as Williamson and Scarlett could tell the officers and crew of the destroyer seemed quite unperturbed about the raid, and their ship appeared to be undamaged. After they had eaten the prisoners were bedded down in the wardroom for the rest of the night.

Early next morning they were awakened by the throbbing of the engines and knew that the ship was under way. Along with other units of the fleet the *Fulmine* was being moved into the inner harbour. Within an hour the destroyer was berthed alongside the dockyard in the Mar Piccolo, and the airmen were informed that they were to be taken ashore.

Blindfolded, they were led over the gangway and driven to the headquarters of the local Carabinieri. There the blindfolds were removed and, one at a time, they were escorted into a room to be interrogated by a naval captain, assisted by an interpreter.

Williamson was questioned first. He felt nervous and apprehensive. After all, the British had just knocked hell out of Mussolini's biggest and most important naval base and there was no telling what the Fascists might do in reprisal.

He need not have worried.

The captain he found to be a charming man, who offered the prisoner a chair, a glass of beer and a cigarette. Cautiously Williamson accepted all three.

'Now I am going to ask you some questions,' smiled the Italian. 'You need not answer them if you don't want to.'

This appeared to be an odd sort of approach, but at least there appeared to be no rubber truncheons or castor oil about. Williamson grinned back and waited to see what was coming.

The first questions were innocuous enough. Name, rank, home address and next of kin.

Then, 'Where did you come from?' asked the captain.

Williamson stiffened in his chair. 'I'm sorry,' he replied. 'But that is one of the questions I cannot answer.'

The captain nodded understandingly. 'I didn't think you would,' he said surprisingly.

For a few moments the two Italians conferred together and

Williamson heard the word Crete mentioned. Perhaps they thought that the raiders had come from a base on that island.

Presently the captain turned again to the pilot and asked if there had been three men in his aircraft.

As Williamson hesitated over his reply, the Italian hastily added, 'The only reason I ask is that if there was a third man in your crew he is probably floating about in the harbour. If we could find him we would give him a military funeral.'

Williamson saw no harm then in confirming that he and his observer were in fact the sole members of their aircrew.

After Scarlett's interrogation, which followed the same lines as that of his companion, the two were kept under guard in police headquarters.

That night the RAF raided Taranto.

The British airmen were conducted down to an air raid shelter. As he entered Williamson glanced round and observed, much to his alarm, that the place was full of Italian sailors. 'Look out, he warned Scarlett, 'there's bound to be trouble.

Instead, to their astonishment, they found themselves being treated as honoured guests. They were given the only two chairs in the shelter and plied with cigarettes. Presently one of the Italians who possessed a good tenor voice began to sing, and his comrades joined in. Before the end of the raid all hands, British and Italians together, were bawling *Tipperary* at the tops of their voices!

The next night there was another raid alert, and once again the two British airmen were taken to a shelter. This time they were followed down by an elegant, wasp-waisted Italian Army officer accompanied by an orderly carrying a silver salver, upon which stood several glasses of Cointreau. With a flashing smile and a graceful bow the officer invited Williamson and Scarlett to partake of the drinks with him.

But if this was intended as a gesture in the grand manner to present to the British airmen an example of Italian coolness under bombing it was rather spoiled by the fact that the raid that night was upon Bari, some forty miles away! Nevertheless they thoroughly enjoyed the liqueur.

However, their confinement in the police station at Taranto soon came to an end and they were sent north by train to Venice. After several weeks there they were transferred to a prisoner-of-war camp at Sulmona. In 1943, following the Italian surrender, the gallant crew of Swordfish L.4A were moved to Hitler's Reich and spent the rest of the war in a German *oflag*.

CHAPTER XIII

A GREAT VICTORY

WHILE Cunningham and his fleet were still on the way back to Alexandria, rumours about the attack on Taranto began to spread like wildfire. The swift reaction of the Fascist propaganda machine was itself a significant hint to foreign observers that the British Navy had accomplished something vastly more important than a mere nuisance raid on Italy's chief naval base.

The admission that 'one unit had been badly damaged was immediately discounted as a deliberate understatement. Fascist propaganda was undoubtedly trying to soften a severe blow for the Italian people and to save face abroad.

The eyes and ears of the free world were turned to London. What would the British Admiralty have to say?

But at first the Admiralty was itself unable to obtain a clear picture of what had happened. The signals which had passed between the Vice-Admiral, Malta, and the fleet, disclosing the results of the detailed examination of Whiteley's reconnaissance pictures, had been repeated to Whitehall, but parts of the messages were unintelligible when received in London. The admiralty petulantly complained to Malta that the signals had not been properly coded, and there was a distinct flavour of scepticism about their request for a repetition.

Was it certain. Their Lordships demanded to know that the enemy ships reported as being aground were really listed over, or might it not be possible that this was merely an impression conveyed by oblique photographs?

There was no scepticism now at Malta, however. An exhaustive interpretation had been made of the aerial photographs, and a prompt and comprehensive reply to the Admiralty left little room for doubt as to the magnitude of the blow which had been struck by the Fleet Air Arm.

This message gave details of the original berthing positions of the Italian battleships, the positions to which they had been moved since the attack, and an assessment of their present condition. From a cautious appraisal of the data thus supplied the conservative-minded Admiralty experts were at last convinced that something approaching a considerable victory indeed appeared to have been achieved.

First to be told the news outside the Admiralty was the King himself, who received the jubilant First Sea Lord together with the equally jubilant Prime Minister on that same day, November 12th. With his wealth of experience at the Admiralty, Churchill did not need to be reminded of the far-reaching effects this massive stroke would have on the naval situation in the Mediterranean.

Not only that, the navy had come up with a victory which would provide a sorely needed stimulus for the nation at a time in Britain's history when the outlook had never been blacker.

In their six o'clock news bulletin on the evening of November 12th the BBC quoted a brief Reuter message in which the Italians admitted that a raid had taken place on Taranto; but this by itself was scarcely sufficient to arouse more than a faint interest in British listeners. Next morning, however, the newspapers headlined the report, and whetted the appetites of their readers by hinting that some surprising news would undoubtedly be forthcoming when the Mediterranean fleet returned to Alexandria.

On the afternoon of the 13th, Churchill, who had been given all the facts so far received by the Admiralty, rose to his feet in the Commons.

'I have some news for the House,' he began with a deadpan expression on his face. Then, after a tantalising pause, he grinned impishly as he added, 'It is good news!'

He told the expectant members, packed tightly on the crowded benches, that the strength of the Italian battle fleet was six battleships, but that in consequence of the Fleet Air Arm's stroke against Mussolini's naval stronghold only three of them remained afloat. In his own inimitable way he related the dramatic story of the action at Taranto.

'The result,' he declared, 'affects decisively the balance of naval power in the Mediterranean, and also carries with it reactions upon the naval situation in every quarter of the globe. I feel sure the House will regard these results as highly satisfactory and as reflecting the greatest credit upon the Admiralty and upon Admiral Cunningham, the Commander-in-Chief in the Mediterranean, and above all on our pilots of the Fleet Air Arm who, like their brothers in the RAF, continue to render their country services of the highest order.'

Earlier the BBC's one o'clock news had included a graphic

three hundred-word communique issued by the Admiralty which, as the result of further enquiries made of the Vice-Admiral, Malta, gave more details than had been signalled from Malta to the *Illustrious* and Admiral Cunningham on the evening of the 12th. This announced that in addition to a *Littorio* and a *Cavour*-class battleship having been crippled, it was probable that a second *Cavour* had also been severely damaged.

The nation was thrilled.

Even more spice was added to the story when it became known that on the same day that the Fleet Air Arm had been preparing to attack Taranto, the Italian Air Force, at the express wish of Mussolini, had been graciously permitted by Hitler to take part in a raid on this country. Italian bombers, escorted by about sixty fighters, attempted to attack our convoys in the Medway. Eight bombers and five fighters were shot down by the RAF. It was the first and last time that the Regia Aeronautica ventured to appear over Britain. They might have been better employed, commented Churchill ironically, in defending their fleet at Taranto.

After the nine o'clock news that evening Mr A. V. Alexander the First Lord of the Admiralty, went to the microphone to pay a glowing tribute to the Fleet Air Arm.

The numerical superiority of the Italian battle fleet, he said, had now been reduced to inferiority. For reasons best known to themselves, he commented scornfully, the Italians had not sought to exploit that superiority from the outset, but had remained immobile behind the defences of their principal harbour. Within this inglorious shelter their battle fleet had suffered a defeat which could only have been redeemed in the public view if that fleet had shown itself willing to accept battle at sea.

This great victory, he went on, would hearten free people everywhere. It was a blow struck in support of our gallant Greek ally. It would cheer them and depress the boastful and opportunist Mussolini who, having waited to enter the war until he thought he was sure of the spoils of victory without fighting, must now know that he was going to be beaten.

The attack at Taranto, said the First Lord, was carried out in moonlight in the face of strong anti-aircraft defences, including a balloon barrage. That it was pressed home so successfully with the loss of only two planes, the crews of which seemed to have been made prisoner, was further evidence of the resoluteness and daring of the whole operation.

The press hastily prepared sketch maps of Taranto, and

combed their files for pictures of Admiral Cunningham and his ships with which to embellish splash stories of the action as soon as further news should come in from Alexandria. In the meanwhile their naval correspondents attempted in various ways to analyse and interpret for their avid readers the possible effects of this remarkable exploit which had been accomplished by a hitherto unregarded arm of the Royal Navy.

Said *The Times*: 'This brilliant victory changes the naval situation – and perhaps the political situation – to an extent which is difficult to over-estimate. It is true that none of the Italian ships is reported to be sunk; of this advantage at least an admiral whose fleet remains anchored in sheltered waters cannot be deprived, but to refloat them and render them fit for service again will require many months of industrious work.

'In the meantime Italy's effective strength in battleships is reduced to three and the balance in the Mediterranean, over-turned by the defection of the French fleet, is fully restored. Such a decisive defeat inflicted upon the Italian Navy immediately after reverses at the hands of the Greeks should go far towards dispelling the aura of Axis invincibility throughout the Mediterranean countries, with incalculable effect upon their future policy.

'The congratulations and gratitude of the nation are due in their fullest measure to the Fleet Air Arm, who have won a great victory in the largest operation in which they have yet been engaged against enemy ships, and to Sir Andrew Cunningham, who is the first flag officer to handle the new weapon on such a scale, and has used it triumphantly.

There was much more to come in similar vein. Taranto had driven the first sizeable nail into Mussolini's coffin, and full advantage was taken of the opportunity to hammer it firmly home.

At seven o'clock on the morning of November 14th the Mediterranean Fleet entered harbour at Alexandria, where a horde of news-hungry pressmen waited to greet the ships. One of the first visitors to the *Illustrious* was that former sailor-airman, Air Chief Marshal Longmore, AOC Middle East, who made a special journey from his headquarters in Cairo to go on board the carrier and congratulate the aircrews.

Felicitous signals poured in. Chief among them was a special message from the King addressed to Admiral Cunningham. 'The recent successful operations of the fleet under your command have been a source of pride and gratification to all at home,' signalled His Majesty. 'Please convey my warm congratulations to the Mediterranean Fleet, and in particular to the Fleet Air Arm, on their brilliant exploit against Italian warships at Taranto.'

Air Chief Marshal Sir Charles Portal, Chief of the Air Staff, sent his heartiest congratulations on a 'magnificent show.'

From the Fifth Sea Lord, the Admiralty Board Member in charge of naval aviation, came a message saying, 'I am eager that my congratulations and those of naval air personnel at home should be conveyed to the Fleet Air Arm engaged at Taranto. The RAF Station at Gosport which has long been connected with aircraft torpedo development and the training of torpedo pilots also wishes to add its congratulations.'

'We are thrilled with your success at Taranto,' signalled the RAF from Cairo, to which message Lyster sent a graceful acknowledgment of the navy's appreciation of the excellent photographic work of the RAF, 'without which Taranto could not have been attacked'.

Wrote the First Sea Lord to Admiral Cunningham: 'Just before the news of Taranto the Cabinet were down in the dumps, but Taranto had a most amazing effect on them!'

And in case Mussolini was thinking of retaliating in kind, the Commander-in-Chief told Boyd and Lyster: 'After the hate you must have engendered and the heavy toll you have taken of the Italians, I think it would be unwise to place the *Illustrious* in dock during full moon period!'

The Americans were almost equally delighted to learn of the spectacular achievement of the Royal Navy's air arm, and Churchill kept President Roosevelt, recently re-elected for his third term of office, fully informed.

In Imperial Navy Headquarters at Tokyo other naval strategists studied this unparalleled example of economy of force with a sinister interest. Adepts at assimilation, the Japanese thirteen months later were to employ an almost identical method of attack against the American fleet at Pearl Harbour.

Taranto had in fact brought about a radical change in the future conduct of naval warfare. Aircraft had now become the fists of the fleet, far out-reaching the largest calibre gun.

Wrote Captain Boyd in a tailpiece to his official report of the operation: 'Although the proper function of the Fleet Air Arm may perhaps be the operation of aircraft against the enemy in the open sea, it has been demonstrated before and repeated in no uncertain fashion by this success, that the ability to strike unexpectedly is conferred by the Fleet Air Arm. It is often felt that this Arm, which has had a long struggle with adverse opinions, and its unspectacular aircraft, is underestimated in its power. It is hoped that this victory will be considered a suitable reward to those whose work and faith in the Fleet Air Arm has made it possible.'

Studying the plan of Taranto and its defences in his news-paper at home, a certain British scientist who had been a friend of Boyd while the latter was at the Admiralty, could not repress a shudder as he mentally pictured the hazards through which the Swordfish crews of the *Illustrious* had had to fly to drop their torpedoes.

'If it had been possible for you to warn me that this attack was to have been made,' he told Boyd long afterwards, 'I would have made you a bouncing bomb which your boys could have dropped with much less risk.'

Three years after Taranto nineteen RAF Lancasters, led by Wing Commander Guy Gibson, used just such a lethal novelty with devastating effect against the Möhne and Eder Dams in Germany.

The scientist's name was Dr Barnes Wallis.

Although none of the Italian ships was irreparably damaged at Taranto, they were temporarily out of the war – one com-pletely, since the *Cavour* was never again rendered fit for service – and the Italians were forced to move the undamaged units of their fleet north to Naples.

Not only that, the use by the British of the Duplex pistol with which their aircraft torpedoes were armed, caused them to overhaul the underwater protection of their capital ships. Double, and even treble, bottoms were no longer sufficient.

Although the *Littorio* was a newer and more powerful vessel than the *Cavour*-class battleships, it might be wondered why she could have been hit by three torpedoes and still remain afloat, while her more elderly consorts had been far more severely damaged by only one torpedo in each case. The answer, was, of course, that the torpedoes fired at the two latter ships had not actually struck them, but exploded magnetically beneath the ships' hulls. Since water is incompressible, the effects of the explosions were considerably more violent.

The Italian Navy was still free to operate in the central Medi-terranean, but only by coming south through the Straits of Messina. In these confined waters Squadron Leader Whiteley and his gallant successors at Malta were able to keep a closer watch on them.

For Cunningham the fruits of the Taranto victory speedily became apparent. The threat of attack on his convoys to Greece and Crete was greatly diminished, with consequent easing of the strain on the British fleet. This relief was in fact so marked that shortly aftrwards it actually became possible to reduce our naval strength in the Mediterranean. The veteran battleships *Malaya* and *Ramilles* were both sent back to the United Kingdom for employment elsewhere.

For Mussolini the results of Taranto were more lasting and far reaching. On land the Greeks bloodied his nose, and soon afterwards General Wavell threw Graziani and his army out of Egypt. Two months later the Italians in the Sudan and East Africa were forced on to the defensive, and by early summer the following year had been defeated.

The Duce bellowed to Hitler for help, and thereafter Italy found herself relegated to the ignominious role of junior partner in the Axis. Although there were sombre times ahead for the British fleet in the Mediterranean, the intervention of the Germans to pull Mussolini's chestnuts out of the fire eventually led to their first full-scale military defeat in North Africa, and thus inevitably to the final downfall of the Third Reich.

But this was still a long way into the future.

Despite the acclaim with which the victory at Taranto had been received in Britain, recognition of the men who had brought it about was astonishingly tardy and meagre.

In the Supplement to the *London Gazette* of December 20th, 1940, it was announced that Hale and Williamson, the strike leaders, had been appointed Companions of the Distinguished Service Order, and Carline and Scarlett, their navigators, awarded the Distinguished Service Cross. DSCs were also awarded to Patch and Goodwin.

And that was all!

The ship's company of the *Illustrious* were hurt and indignant and they vented their feelings by ripping down the noticeboard copies of the Fleet Orders in which the announcement of the awards had been published. Williamson and Hale, they considered, ought to have been recommended for the Victoria Cross, and the rest of the aircrews should have received immediate awards of an only slightly less distinguished decoration for gallantry. 'After all, that's what would have happened in the

RAF,' they argued, 'why not in the RN?'

Nor was their disappointment assuaged to any appreciable extent when in the New Year's Honours List published on January 1st, 1941, Admiral Lyster was awarded the CB, and Captains Boyd and Bridge, of the *Illustrious* and *Eagle* respectively, the CBE.

In fact it was not until the following May – no less than six months after the operation – that a further list of awards was published.

DSOs were awarded to Clifford and Going. Kemp, Torrens-Spence, Lea, Macauley, Kiggell, Hamilton, Janvrin, Sutton, Bailey, Jones, Neale, Weekes and Wray received the DSC, and Sparke was given a Bar to the DSC he had won earlier. Eighteen others, including Swayne, Forde, Maund, Sarra, Bayly and Slaughter, were mentioned in despatches.

Even then there was considered to be a glaring omission in this belated and niggardly list. Not one officer or rating on the maintenance and non-flying staffs of the *Illustrious* who had worked so tirelessly to get the aircraft into the air received any recognition whatever.

It seemed to many in the Fleet Air Arm that the striking demonstration of the immense potential of air power afloat which had been staged by the men of Taranto was even now being acknowledged grudgingly and with reluctance. Yet it was soon to be proved beyond doubt that the battle of Taranto – for the Fleet Air Arm regards this as a 'battle' and not a mere raid – marked as decisive a turning point in naval warfare as had the action at Trafalgar more than a century earlier. It was the end of an era and the beginning of another, in which sea battles would be fought without the rival fleets even sighting each other.

Pearl Harbour, Colombo and Trincomalee, and later the actions by the Americans fought against the Japanese in the Pacific at Tulagi, the Coral Sea, Midway and Leyte Gulf, all undoubtedly stemmed from that memorable night in 1940 when a score of obsolete British aircraft, none of which remained in the target area for more than three or four minutes, inflicted more damage upon an enemy fleet than was suffered by the might of the German Navy in daylight at the Battle of Jutland.

CHAPTER XIV

AFTERMATH

TRAGICALLY enough, one-third of the aircrews who took part in the battle of Taranto never lived to know that their gallantry was eventually recognised. For some of these the arrival in Sicily of the Luftwaffe as part of Hitler's response to his fellow dictator's call for aid, following Taranto and the Italian defeats in Greece and North Africa, was to bring about their own destruction.

Early in 1941 Admiral Cunningham staged another important convoy operation in the Mediterranean. Although much less complex and involving fewer ships than Operation MB8, it nevertheless required the deployment of almost his entire naval strength, and the services in an escorting role of Admiral Somerville s Force H from Gibraltar. Appropriately enough, perhaps, in view of the massive numbers of warships engaged, the operation was code-named 'Excess'.

The main purpose of Operation Excess was to pass through the Mediterranean a convoy of four fast merchantmen, three of which were laden with urgently needed stores for Greece, and one for Malta. As he did in Operation MB8, Cunningham also took the opportunity to despatch two more merchantmen laden with supplies from Alexandria to Malta at the same time. Two of his cruisers, the *Gloucester* and *Southampton*, also acted as transports to take troops to the island. The fast convoy from the west was to be escorted by Force H from Gibraltar as far as the Pantellaria Channel, where it would be taken over for onward passage by Admiral Cunningham.

Force H comprised the battle-cruiser *Renown*, the battleship *Malaya*, the aircraft-carrier *Ark Royal*, the cruiser *Sheffield* and the best part of a flotilla of destroyers. Another cruiser, the *Bonaventure*, with four destroyers acted as close escort for the merchantmen.

From Alexandria Cunningham sailed in the *Warspite*, accompanied by the *Valiant* and *Illustrious*. The troop-carrying cruisers under the command of Rear-Admiral E. de F. Renouf sailed ahead of the main body.

All went well up to the time of turnover of the eastbound convoy, which passed under the protection of Admiral Renouf on January 9th, the troops his ships had been transporting having been safely disembarked in Malta on the previous day. An Italian air attack had been beaten off by aircraft from the *Ark Royal*, and an Italian destroyer sunk in a dawn brush with the convoy escorts. A few hours later Cunningham joined up with Renouf, and the fleet shaped course eastwards.

But from the time they left Alexandria Admiral Cunningham's ships had been persistently shadowed. A new and more deadly threat from the air had been alerted and was even now preparing to strike.

Soon after mid-day on January 10th two Italian torpedo-bombers came in low to attack the *Illustrious*. They dropped their torpedoes at a range of four hundred yards under a hail of fire from the carrier's close-range weapons. Boyd swung his ship round to meet the attack, and the enemy torpedoes passed harmlessly astern. Twelve minutes later the skies above the fleet were filled with enemy aircraft, both German and Italian.

More than twenty-five Ju.87s and Ju.88s made for the *Illustrious*, and came screaming down on her just as the last of a batch of Fulmar fighters was soaring up from her flight deck. A moment later it seemed to watchers in the other ships that the carrier was completely obliterated in a vast upsurge of smoke and spray from bursting bombs.

Her two foremost pom-pom guns were destroyed and her radar smashed in the first salvo. The after lift, which was on the way up to the flight deck with a fighter on it, was blown into shapelessness and plane and pilot vanished completely. Splinters from this bomb, which was a thousand-pounder, put eight of the after 4.5-inch guns out of action and started a fire in the hangar. The Germans were out to avenge Taranto - and they all but succeeded.

At one-thirty in the afternoon high-level bombers attacked the carrier with equal skill and determination. One heavy bomb plunged through the armoured flight deck and out through the ship's side before exploding. Blast from the explosion buckled the foremost lift and started more fires among the Swordfish in the hangar.

Soon after four o'clock fifteen dive-bombers came in remorselessly to pound the punch-drunk *Illustrious* still further. Again they scored a direct hit on the flight deck with a 1,000-lb. bomb. This smashed through to the hangar and exploded, killing or wounding everybody in the wardroom and starting a third fire. Flames spurting from broken petrol pipes set off some of the ready-use ammunition to add to the terrifying chaos below.

A few minutes later another heavy bomb hurtled down the after-lift well and its explosion wrecked the steering compartment. The ship started charging round in circles until Boyd managed to regain control and began to steer by the use of the main engines alone.

While the blazing carrier was limping towards the doubtful shelter of Malta, with the ship's company working like demons to keep her afloat, yet another attack developed, this time by torpedo-bombers. At one stage in the action it was reported to Boyd that a fire was raging above one of the remaining magazines, and permission was asked to flood the compartment.

Boyd was now placed in a terrible predicament. Ammunition was running low. All that remained would undoubtedly be needed to beat off fresh attacks. Yet if the fire could not be checked and the magazine exploded the damage caused might well be mortal. Boyd decided that he must take the risk, and grimly he refused permission for the magazine to be flooded. He could not leave the ship without any means of defence.

'After I gave the order,' he said, 'I walked away with my empty pipe clenched tightly in my jaws to stop my teeth from chattering with fright!'

But that was not the impression he conveyed to the battle-shocked men of the *Illustrious*. Afterwards one of these, in a letter home, thus described the deadly air assault which had so severely damaged the carrier, and the apparent imperturbability of her captain:

'We had a bit of a rough time the other day with a convoy off Malta. The ship was on fire and I thought we weren't going to make it. But when I looked up on the bridge I saw the Skipper standing there smoking his pipe as cool as you please, and I knew we were going to be all right.'

After dark on the evening of January 10th the crippled carrier limped into Malta's Grand Harbour, and the sad work of checking up the dead and wounded commenced.

The casualties totalled eighty-three officers and men killed, sixty seriously wounded and forty slightly wounded.

Of the Swordfish aircrews, Lieutenant Kemp of 815 Squadron who flew L.4K in the first strike at Taranto had been killed instantly by the bomb that exploded in the hangar.

Skelton and Perkins, pilot and observer respectively of

Swordfish L.4F, who had bombed the oil tanks in the second attack, were both killed. Perkin's end had been peculiarly tragic. He had first been knocked unconscious by the explosion of the bomb which wrecked the wardroom, and then drowned in the subsequent flooding. Skelton died of wounds two days after the attack.

Clifford, who, with Going, had carried out the solitary bomb attack on the Mar Piccolo at Taranto half an hour after the second strike had left the scene, was last seen in a wounded condition near the quarterdeck of the *Illustrious* during the height of the bombing. Subsequently he disappeared, and it was assumed that he had been blown over the side during a later attack.

Going himself, while working below with the damage-control parties, had had a leg blown off by the bomb which wrecked the carrier's steering compartment.

Sub-Lieutenant Mardel-Ferreira, who had been navigator to Forde, his fellow sub-lieutenant, in Swordfish L.4H, was one of those who were killed outright in the bombing, Tony Wray, navigator and observer for Macauley in L.4K in the first strike on Taranto, succumbed to the wounds he had received on the evening of January 11th. Boyd was with him at the end. His last unselfish words were addressed to his captain. 'I'm glad you got the ship in safely, sir,' he said, and died.

Morford, whose overload petrol tank fell off on the night of the Taranto raid and thus prevented him from continuing with the second strike, was terribly burned in the bombing. Later by the miracle of plastic surgery he was given almost a new face.

All the dead were avenged on the same day by their comrades. At least seven of the enemy planes were shot down by Fulmars from the *Illustrious*, which had landed in Malta to refuel and re-arm; and another six by the carrier's own gunfire.

Subsequently eleven more of the original members of the Taranto aircrews lost their lives. Among these were Sparke, who transferred to fighters and perished in a collision with a German aircraft; Macauley, the gay and heedless, who crashed into the sea when the wings of his Swordfish came off in a vertical power dive; Hamilton and Weekes who were shot down in an attack on Leros; and Maund, killed while on operations from Malta.

Of the crew of Swordfish E.4H who had been shot down at Taranto, only the body of Lieutenant Bayly was recovered. He was buried with full naval honours by the Italians at Taranto, but after the war the coffin was removed and reinterred in the Imperial War Graves cemetery at Bari. Slaughter's name appears on the Fleet Air Arm Memorial at Lee on Solent with the rest of those wartime naval airmen who have no known grave.

As for the *Illustrious*, the bombing she had undergone during Operation Excess injured her very severely, but it by no means put her out of the fight. For the next twelve days she remained at Malta while her company strove to make her seaworthy. Every day she was dive-bombed by the Luftwaffe, but they only managed to score one direct hit on their target.

On the evening of January 24th she left Malta after dark, unobserved and headed for Alexandria at 24 knots, which port she reached safely. After further patching up in the dockyard there she was sailed via the Cape for Norfolk, Virginia, in the USA. There she underwent an eight-months refit, coming, for part of the time, under the command of Captain (now Admiral of the Fleet Earl) Lord Louis Mountbatten. But before he could take her to sea he was appointed to the post of Chief of Combined Operations.

In March 1942, the *Illustrious* joined Britain's Eastern Fleet as the flagship of her first captain, Denis Boyd, who by then had become Rear-Admiral, Aircraft-Carriers, Eastern Fleet, where she took part in the Madagascar landings.

Subsequently she was present at the Salerno landings, and in 1943 rejoined the Eastern Fleet. Later as one of the carriers in the British Pacific Fleet she operated off Palembang and Formosa against the Japanese, and helped to provide air cover for the American invasion of Okinawa.

After the war the *Illustrious* was employed in home waters as Trials and Training Carrier, and later as Trials Carrier only, testing new aircraft, equipment and techniques. In 1951 she transported troops to the Middle East for operations in the Suez Canal Zone.

Finally in 1956 the gallant old ship was scrapped.

Today there is no *Illustrious* in the British Navy. But if and when her successor appears she will carry one battle honour on her scroll that to the Fleet Air Arm will always remain supreme – Taranto.

THE END

THE RED BERET

by
Hilary St. George Saunders

This is the story of Arnhem, Bruneval, the Ardennes, Normandy, the crossing of the Rhine. It is the story of the Red Devils, the most heroic band of daredevils any war has ever produced.

NEW ENGLISH LIBRARY

NEL BESTSELLERS

Crime

T013 332	CLOUDS OF WITNESS	*Dorothy L. Sayers* 40p
T016 307	THE UNPLEASANTNESS AT THE BELLONA CLUB	
		Dorothy L. Sayers 40p
W003 011	GAUDY NIGHT	*Dorothy L. Sayers* 40p
T010 457	THE NINE TAILORS	*Dorothy L. Sayers* 35p
T012 484	FIVE RED HERRINGS	*Dorothy L. Sayers* 40p
T015 556	MURDER MUST ADVERTISE	*Dorothy L. Sayers* 40p
T014 398	STRIDING FOLLY	*Dorothy L. Sayers* 30p

Fiction

T013 944	CRUSADER'S TOMB	*A. J. Cronin* 60p
T013 936	THE JUDAS TREE	*A. J. Cronin* 50p
T015 386	THE NORTHERN LIGHT	*A. J. Cronin* 50p
T016 544	THE CITADEL	*A. J. Cronin* 75p
T016 919	THE SPANISH GARDENER	*A. J. Cronin* 40p
T014 088	BISHOP IN CHECK	*Adam Hall* 30p
T015 467	PAWN IN JEOPARDY	*Adam Hall* 30p
T015 130	THE MONEY MAKER	*John J. McNamara Jr.* 50p
T014 932	YOU NICE BASTARD	*G. F. Newman* 50p
T009 769	THE HARRAD EXPERIMENT	*Robert H. Rimmer* 40p
T012 522	THURSDAY MY LOVE	*Robert H. Rimmer* 40p
T013 820	THE DREAM MERCHANTS	*Harold Robbins* 75p
T018 105	THE CARPETBAGGERS	*Harold Robbins* 95p
T016 560	WHERE LOVE HAS GONE	*Harold Robbins* 75p
T013 707	THE ADVENTURERS	*Harold Robbins* 80p
T006 743	THE INHERITORS	*Harold Robbins* 60p
T009 467	STILETTO	*Harold Robbins* 30p
T015 289	NEVER LEAVE ME	*Harold Robbins* 40p
T016 579	NEVER LOVE A STRANGER	*Harold Robbins* 75p
T011 798	A STONE FOR DANNY FISHER	*Harold Robbins* 60p
T015 874	79 PARK AVENUE	*Harold Robbins* 60p
T011 461	THE BETSY	*Harold Robbins* 75p
T010 201	RICH MAN, POOR MAN	*Irwin Shaw* 80p
T018 148	THE PLOT	*Irving Wallace* 90p
T009 718	THE THREE SIRENS	*Irving Wallace* 75p
T013 340	SUMMER OF THE RED WOLF	*Morris West* 50p

Historical

T013 731	KNIGHT WITH ARMOUR	*Alfred Duggan* 40p
T013 758	THE LADY FOR RANSOM	*Alfred Duggan* 40p
T015 297	COUNT BOHEMOND	*Alfred Duggan* 50p
T010 279	MASK OF APOLLO	*Mary Renault* 50p
T015 580	THE CHARIOTEER	*Mary Renault* 50p
T010 988	BRIDE OF LIBERTY	*Frank Yerby* 30p
T014 045	TREASURE OF PLEASANT VALLEY	*Frank Yerby* 35p
T015 602	GILLIAN	*Frank Yerby* 50p

Science Fiction

T014 576	THE INTERPRETER	*Brian Aldiss* 30p
T015 017	EQUATOR	*Brian Aldiss* 30p
T014 347	SPACE RANGER	*Isaac Asimov* 30p
T015 491	PIRATES OF THE ASTEROIDS	*Isaac Asimov* 30p
T016 951	THUVIA MAID OF MARS	*Edgar Rice Burroughs* 30p
T016 331	THE CHESSMEN OF MARS	*Edgar Rice Burroughs* 40p

T011 682	ESCAPE ON VENUS	*Edgar Rice Burroughs*	40p
T013 537	WIZARD OF VENUS	*Edgar Rice Burroughs*	30p
T009 696	GLORY ROAD	*Robert Heinlein*	40p
T010 856	THE DAY AFTER TOMORROW	*Robert Heinlein*	30p
T016 900	STRANGER IN A STRANGE LAND	*Robert Heinlein*	75p
T011 844	DUNE	*Frank Herbert*	75p
T012 298	DUNE MESSIAH	*Frank Herbert*	40p
T015 211	THE GREEN BRAIN	*Frank Herbert*	30p

War

T013 367	DEVIL'S GUARD	*Robert Elford*	50p
T013 324	THE GOOD SHEPHERD	*C. S. Forester*	35p
T011 755	TRAWLERS GO TO WAR	*Lund & Ludlam*	40p
T015 505	THE LAST VOYAGE OF GRAF SPEE	*Michael Powell*	30p
T015 661	JACKALS OF THE REICH	*Ronald Seth*	30p
T012 263	FLEET WITHOUT A FRIEND	*John Vader*	30p

Western

T016 994	No. 1 EDGE – THE LONER	*George G. Gilman*	30p
T016 986	No. 2 EDGE – TEN THOUSAND DOLLARS AMERICAN		
		George G. Gilman	30p
T017 613	No. 3 EDGE – APACHE DEATH	*George G. Gilman*	30p
T017 001	No. 4 EDGE – KILLER'S BREED	*George G. Gilman*	30p
T016 536	No. 5 EDGE – BLOOD ON SILVER	*George G. Gilman*	30p
T017 621	No. 6 EDGE – THE BLUE, THE GREY AND THE RED		
		George G. Gilman	30p
T014 479	No. 7 EDGE – CALIFORNIA KILLING	*George G. Gilman*	30p
T015 254	No. 8 EDGE – SEVEN OUT OF HELL	*George G. Gilman*	30p
T015 475	No. 9 EDGE – BLOODY SUMMER	*George G. Gilman*	30p
T015 769	No. 10 EDGE – VENGEANCE IS BLACK	*George G. Gilman*	30p

General

T011 763	SEX MANNERS FOR MEN	*Robert Chartham*	30p
W002 531	SEX MANNERS FOR ADVANCED LOVERS	*Robert Chartham*	25p
W002 835	SEX AND THE OVER FORTIES	*Robert Chartham*	30p
T010 732	THE SENSUOUS COUPLE	*Dr. 'C'*	25p

Mad

S004 708	VIVA MAD!	30p
S004 676	MAD'S DON MARTIN COMES ON STRONG	30p
S004 816	MAD'S DAVE BERG LOOKS AT SICK WORLD	30p
S005 078	MADVERTISING	30p
S004 987	MAD SNAPPY ANSWERS TO STUPID QUESTIONS	30p

NEL P.O. BOX 11, FALMOUTH, TR10 9EN, CORNWALL
    Please send cheque or postal order. Allow 10p to cover postage and packing on one book plus 4p for each additional book.

Name ....

Address..

    ....

Title ....
(SEPTEMBER)